THE
BLACK
PENTECOSTAL
CHURCH:
MY VIEW FROM THE PEW

SHARON D. SMITH

WESTBOW
PRESS®
A DIVISION OF THOMAS NELSON
& ZONDERVAN

Edited by Robert Kidd of EditFast, Canada

Book Cover artwork titled: "Morning Prayer" by Ray Ellis.
Compass Prints, Inc./Ray Ellis Gallery, Savannah, GA

WestBow Press books may be ordered through booksellers or by contacting:

WestBow Press
A Division of Thomas Nelson & Zondervan
1663 Liberty Drive
Bloomington, IN 47403
www.westbowpress.com
1 (866) 928-1240

ISBN: 978-1-5127-4507-8 (sc)
ISBN: 978-1-5127-4509-2 (hc)
ISBN: 978-1-5127-4508-5 (e)

Library of Congress Control Number: 2016909233

Print information available on the last page.

WestBow Press rev. date: 06/14/2016

SCRIPTURE PAGE

*"Who is left among you that saw this house in her first glory? And how do ye see it now? Is it not in your eyes in comparison of it as nothing? Yet now be strong . . . all ye people of the land, saith the L*ORD*, and work: for I am with you, saith the L*ORD *of hosts. . . . The glory of this latter house shall be greater than of the former, saith the L*ORD *of hosts: and in this place will I give peace, saith the L*ORD *of hosts."* – Haggai 2:3, 4, & 9

DEDICATION PAGE

This book is dedicated to the many prayer warriors who tarried at the altars with souls who sought salvation and deliverance.

I had a dream and in the dream I saw people standing around the altar praying over my mother who was kneeling, crying and praying to the Lord. A voice told me, "It was the effectual, fervent prayers of the prayer warriors around the altar in the 1960s that you, your children and grandchildren are saved today."

CONTENTS

INTRODUCTION

Muddling over what to name this book, I had two titles in mind; one was "The Evolution of the Black Pentecostal Church," which might have people thinking I am writing about the history of the Pentecostal Church. That is not what I am trying to do. The other title in my attempts at being more provocative was "What in the World Happened to the Black Pentecostal Church?" That title was a little too partial as I want to have a discussion, not an argument. By writing this book, I aim to bring to the forefront the plausibility that the Pentecostal Church is severely reducing its impact on the world by embracing the social norms of society today.

It is not my intention to condemn or ridicule the church or its leaders, but rather to exchange dialogue by comparing the 'former' church to the 'latter' church from the time period of the 1960s to present day. My view from the pew will begin with my years of comprehension, and that would be from the mid-1960s up to the present. I will attempt to compare the 'former' church to the 'latter' church; the 'former' being the church as I remember it from childhood, and the 'latter' being the church of today.

Now, I am writing from my perception of the church as a little black girl growing up in Harlem, New York. I can only write from what I have experienced and thus compare how the church was then, and how it is now. By the way, you did know there is the black Pentecostal church and the white Pentecostal church? The Rev. Dr. Martin Luther King Jr. once said that 11 a.m. on a Sunday morning is the most segregated hour in this nation (*The Blaze*, Billy Hallowell, 2015). I can only write from my extensive experience of sitting on the pew in the black Pentecostal church.

By exploring the Scriptures alongside the standards of the Pentecostal Church, I endeavor to determine if by enforcing its attenuate rules and regulations, the church is becoming irrelevant in the eyes of society. Some of the changes that have taken place in the Pentecostal Church, over the past fifty years, have come at a rapid pace, according to who you speak to. Writing my own personal experiences in the Pentecostal Church, my view from the pew, I would like to gauge where the Pentecostal Church stands today. While everything is moving so fast, and information is coming at us at a meteoric pace, we, the long-standing members of the Pentecostal Church, should stop and consider the position of the church as it relates to today's events. I am praying as I write that I do not lead anyone astray.

Why would a long-standing church member air the church's dirty laundry to the public? We need to examine the laundry and see if it needs to be washed again. The Word of God says in Ephesians 5:27, *"That he might present it to himself a glorious church, not having spot, or wrinkle, or any such thing; but that it should be holy and without blemish."* After we take a closer look at the problems, we may wish to re-wash, iron, press, and fold the laundry so it will be ready for our soon coming King.

If there are readers of this book who do not attend any church, much less a Pentecostal church, and think the issues this book raises reinforces their resolve to not attend church; my prayer is that the leadership of our churches will revisit some of the decisions and influences we have made in some of our churches. We should endeavor to make the necessary adjustments by the leading of the Lord, and pray that God will restore the power of the Holy Ghost in its sanctuaries. Once the church is in order, when people do come to church, they will experience the free-flowing anointing in the services the way it should be. Oh, how I wish the young people and new converts could feel the power of God moving through an anointed service like we felt it in the 'former' church. The free-flowing spirit moving through a worship service fosters

Salvation, deliverance, healings, revival, and renewal to the repentant hearts. There is nothing on earth like it! This is my prayer.

With all the stress in society—family issues, finances, health and world affairs—we must also consider the state of the church. Will the church remain an essential part of our lives as well as our children's lives? There are people, for various reasons, who believe the church should no longer exist. There are some folks who believe the church is irrelevant. Even the powers that be, some once-revered and respected court judges, have expressed contempt for the Holy Bible. These powerful people consider the Holy Bible 'ancient writings' that should not be literally adhered to, much less carried out in our everyday lives. The enemy of our souls would love for the church to close its doors for good. Based on my years of attendance and observation in the church, I wonder if I could voice my views from the pews. I'm the last person on this earth who would want to sow discord among the brethren. I just wonder if we could just sit and think about what's going on in the church, and consider if we are on the right track.

I recently saw a group of black men dancing across a church pulpit. The men were bouncing up and down and waving one arm in the air. They bent their bodies over and grouped together, still bouncing and waving and chanting. Most of the men were wearing jeans and sneakers, with their shirt tails hanging out, while they bounced in unison. I began to think that, maybe these kinds of dances stem from our African heritage? Perhaps we have it in us to dance and chant together, bounce and sway together as a natural part of our being. On the other hand, these types of dances looked like they came straight from the hip hop and rap artists of today, which we 'former' church-goers called 'the world dances.' Whenever a new dance comes from the hip hop and rap world, the young people want to do it in the church. As I watch these men bounce up and down, doing their new dance, I could not help but wonder, what would happen if the power of the Holy Spirit would blow over them? They would feel fire shoot up in their bones, and they would do more than bounce up and down and wave an arm in the air in unison. Oh Lord, I pray that the young will get to know You in a very real way.

I want us to pray about what we are saying and doing in our churches. Let us see if we are leading our children in the way they *should* go, in order that our children and grandchildren may know the real purpose of the church. For example, would we be correct in saying to our son, "No, baby, it was wrong for the pastor to allow the congregation to watch the Super Bowl football game in the sanctuary." Or, would it have been correct to say, "It was OK the pastor allowed his congregation to watch the Super Bowl football game in the sanctuary because it brought families together." Which answer is the correct answer, Church? This really happened, folks! I thought they were watching the game on screens in, perhaps, one of the overflow rooms. Right in the main sanctuary, people were lounging across the seats in the main sanctuary. Empty cans and cups were strewn everywhere. The game came across three widescreens on the pulpit. It was not enough that worship services were often cut short on Super Bowl Sundays because people wanted to rush home to catch the game. Now, the game is shown right in the church, in the main sanctuary! People gave reasons favoring both answers.

Considering our past, were our elders wrong in the early church to instruct that watching television was a sin? Were they preventing greater sins as exist now? Look at how much is said and seen on the television today. Are we more enlightened now that television has invaded our homes and churches, and we spend more time in front of it instead of in front of the altar?

My mother was Saved, Sanctified and received the Baptism of the Holy Ghost in the Pentecostal Church in 1959. I was raised in the church and was also Saved and Sanctified, but did not receive the gift of the Holy Spirit until twenty years later. Now, after some fifty-four years, I consider myself an expert layperson of the Pentecostal Church. I can talk about the environs of the church before the song "Oh Happy Day" came out, and how the environs of the church have progressed after the song came out.

People who do not understand the Pentecostal Church may initially think of it as the far fringes of religion, because of its strange activities and strict rules. Some may even believe the ministers were putting spells on people, making them act strange—people jumping up and down, rolling on the floors, stammering and speaking in unintelligible words. As it was said down through the decades by people observing all these things, "It doesn't take all of that!"

As a child growing up in the Pentecostal Church back in the 1960s, I was teased and persecuted because my family attended a Pentecostal church. I was called a 'Holy Roller' and 'church girl' and unsparingly ostracized, criticized and ridiculed. As I have written in my second book, *Screen Door: A Memoir*, back in those days, it was not popular to be a born again Christian. We were considered strange people, a peculiar people, who did not participate in extracurricular activities like dancing, going to parties or listening to 'worldly' music. Girls did not wear pants or makeup, and no member of the church used foul language. In society today, all these restrictions are considered 'hang ups' and old-fashioned rules.

As a young person, I was not happy attending a church with such strict rules; however, as an adult, I want the church to exist and be a place of refuge and a place of prayer. I want the church to be as the lyrics of the old gospel song says:

"A glorious church
without spot or wrinkle,
washed in the Blood of the Lamb."

I think the church must remain a place where the weary soul can come before the Lord to worship, find peace, and also to rejoice. To this end, I would love it if the church could be open twenty-four hours a day, seven days a week. It would be wonderful to go into a Pentecostal church anytime, to say a prayer, just like a Catholic congregation can. Unfortunately, in today's society, the expense and now concerns of the homeless and transients coming in, not to pray but to find a place to sleep, hinders that. The church should be a place where the searching heart can find answers and receive the Holy Spirit for guidance and comfort. To condense the church down to becoming just a community center, a homeless shelter or a club, takes away its spirituality and its significance.

In today's society, the enemy of our souls, which is the Devil, wants to take away our freedom of religion. People want us to pray at home and in secret. Not only pray at home, but in our closets, at home. Matthew 6:6 reads: *"But thou, when thou prayest, enter into thy closet, and when thou hast shut thy door, pray to thy Father which is in secret; and thy Father which seeth in secret shall reward thee openly."* Society today commands us to pray out of the public eye, not in the schools, not at graduations, nor on the football field.

Always remember this: The enemy of our souls is a liar and the father of lies (John 8:44). He *cannot* tell the truth, so he cites Scripture falsely, just as he did with Jesus in the wilderness to back up his falsehood. He tells the same lies today. The verse of Matthew 6:6 in no way means a person should go into a literal closet and close the door to pray. It only means, whenever you pray in your heart, God will see it and will answer that prayer openly.

There are many instances in Scripture where Our Lord and Savior Jesus Christ prayed right out in the open. Our Lord and Savior Jesus Christ even taught us how to pray while on the hillside speaking to thousands of people out in the open. Also, the disciples prayed in the streets, at the gate called Beautiful, and in the marketplaces. The enemy of our souls does not want us to pray out in the open, because he will be exposed and he knows there is power in prayer.

In Mark 5:22-42, Jesus was on His way to Jairus's house to pray for his dying daughter, when at the same time, a woman with the "issue of blood" touched Him and was healed. This took place right out in the open. Then in Matthew 8:5-13, after Jesus healed a leper, the centurion asked for prayer for his faithful servant, right out in the open. After that, Jesus healed Peter's mother-in-law—all done while crowds of people were all around.

When I read where Jesus reached down and touched Peter's mother-in-law's hand and the fever left her body, and she immediately received strength to live, I think of the Michelangelo masterpiece *Creation of Adam*, depicting God's finger pointing to the lifeless finger of Adam, giving him life. God only has to point a finger toward us to give us renewed strength and life. Hallelujah!!

I give all those examples to say: though society no longer tolerates prayers in public places because it 'offends' them, we should all have the freedom to pray wherever and whenever we wish. How harmful is a prayer? The harm is, if everyone is praying and the person who does not wish to pray is left out, he is then exposed and revealed as a person who does not pray or who does not believe in Our Lord and Savior Jesus Christ. The enemy of our souls does not wish to be exposed like that. He wants to be clothed in secret and walk among society secretly and quietly dwelling amongst the people, and always trying to change the norms of life. The enemy wants prayers done in secret, quiet, out of earshot so no one can hear the prayers against sins and abominations.

In today's society, what we once considered wrong is now right and what we once considered right is now wrong. What was once unacceptable and immoral in our society, is now accepted and even encouraged. If you want to be current and progressive in today's society, you had better change your belief in the Holy Bible and conform to this world's system.

Here lies the predicament of the church. Are the rules of the church too strict for today's society? Should the church lighten up on its standards? Truthfully, the church has already lowered some of its standards. In this book, I will compare the church in these terms, the *'former'* church, meaning in the past, and the *'latter'* church, meaning today in this present time.

I do not consider myself an authority on what is wrong or right in the church; I am just a pew-viewer who has seen the changes occur, ever so slowly, ever so profoundly. This book will certainly not be an authority on the history of the Pentecostal faith from its beginning, either. To become more familiar on those topics, you can attend Bible College, or take to the Internet and learn of the history of the church and read all about its origins.

My view, for this purpose, is on the relevancy and purpose of the church as it relates to our lives today. Everything the church has taught us and we believed in, was it all for naught? Were the elders and pastors wrong in their teachings of the statutes and standards of the church? Has the church disintegrated into just another place to hang out?

The church, once revered and held in high esteem in people's hearts, now holds no apprehensions for people who are committing sins right in the church. A pastor will have an affair with another man's wife; a husband will kill the pastor because the pastor is having an affair with his wife. Two pregnant girls, pregnant by the same man who attends the same church, and the man will sit comfortably in the pews. A pastor might have two first ladies sitting in the same congregation. There are even graver situations going on in the church today; let your imagination run rampant and, rest assured, it is happening right in the church.

What happened to the fear of God? There are no more standards, no more reverence for the House of God, thus, making all the decrees and standards of non-effect. How did the Pentecostal Church come to this? I can only speak from my view from the pew. My view will be taken from my own personal experiences and observations of the church.

In the church's attempts to keep up with society, to stay current, and to battle that ever-present need to keep people in the pews, the church is losing its special relevance in the lives of people. Hebrews 13:8 reads: *"Jesus Christ the same yesterday, and today, and forever."* If Our Lord and Savior Jesus Christ never changes, why has the church changed? It would be so much easier for everyone concerned if the church just remained a House of Prayer, as our Lord and Savior commanded. Trying to make it a place to please everybody's wants and desires brings confusion; not to mention, the absence of the presence of the Lord.

The 'latter' church (today's church) has changed some of its old rules believing they are too hard, too strict or, some of them, even unnecessary. In my humble opinion, I believe the church should stand strong in its convictions. The church should adhere to the Word of God in all its meaning. If the church conforms to the norms of this world, where can the people turn when they are ready to change? If the church is similar to places like the club, community centers and entertainment arenas, and no life-changing event occurs, then why have a church?

Some may say life-changing events can happen in a club or community center. God's presence can be felt anywhere. Yes, I will give you that, but when you enter into a House of Prayer, and you worship the Lord in His house, and hear the Word of God coming across that sacred desk, your soul receives His heavenly bread, and you are born again, that's life changing. Jesus said, *"Come unto me, all ye that labor and are heavy laden, and I will give you rest"* (Matt. 11:28).

I know there is a deeper meaning; yes, *we*, the *people*, are the church the Lord is coming back for; a church without spot or wrinkle (Eph. 5:27). I am speaking of the place where we worship, which we call the church (Mark 11:17, Matt. 21:13, Luke 19:46). If we conduct our church like a ballroom, dance hall, club house, or community center, then is it a place of worship, holy, unto God? Walking into a church should be different than walking into any other place.

About every ten years someone comes up with a new way of doing things in the church. Someone is always trying to bring the church 'up to date.' It is believed the church cannot be relevant in today's society if it does not change with the times. In the movie *Sister Act*, the Catholic church was cold and empty until Whoopi Goldberg's character, named Sister Mary Clarence, brought in secular songs and jamming beats to entertain the congregants. Then the church's attendance increased, bringing in a lot more young people. At the end of the movie, even the Pope showed up to hear the secular songs (with changed lyrics). The thinking being, unless we conform to the world, the church will die; forget about 'transforming' the world to the ways of God. Romans 12:2 reads: *"And be not conformed to this world: but be ye transformed by the renewing of your mind, that ye may prove what is that good, and acceptable, and perfect, will of God."* It is only by transformation that we will be able to perform the will of God. I believe if the church does not allow the Lord to transform people's hearts and minds, and keeps trying so hard to conform to the ways of society, it will lose its way, and many souls will be lost. As the old church members used to say, "What it takes for Grandma to get saved, it will take for the children, too."

Although I have my own personal thoughts to convey, this does not excuse my writing in a less than accurate or truthful a manner as possible. I do not want to misrepresent my Heavenly Father, my Lord and Savior Jesus Christ. It is essential that I give as accurate an account for everything I write in this book so to keep the sanctity of the House of God, and not lead anyone astray. My perceptions are purely my own, and the way I perceived events and occurrences of church activities is how I am evaluating how we lead and preserve the reverence of the House of God.

I can only speak from my view from the pew; therefore, I am not here to ridicule the church or even to reprimand it. I only dare to speak of what I have observed down through the years, and hope my thoughts help us to ponder how much of the changes are beneficial to our faith. I do want to leave questions in the readers' minds, especially those who love the Pentecostal Church, regarding what should be allowed in the holy House of God. In my opinion, the Pentecostal Church has evolved into something that would be unrecognizable to the old church members who have passed on. The changes in the church are largely due to people becoming more educated and craving to be favorably accepted by the world at large.

When people come into a church, they should prepare themselves accordingly; they should dress for church, have the mindset that a church should be revered and honored. The church should have the ambience of a holy place. People should not walk into the sanctuary of any church popping gum, wearing flip-flops, cursing, and having earphones in their ears blasting sinful music. But these opinions come from an old pew-viewer, and perhaps after reading this book, we might find more like-minded people, or those who feel these opinions too strict, too hard or even unnecessary. Let's look at these views and discuss them.

| C H A P T E R   1 |

Saved, Sanctified, and Filled

Using the colloquial expression of young people today, "back in the day" the average Pentecostal church was headed up by a pastor and an assistant pastor along with a couple of deacons, missionaries, church mothers, ushers, and lay members. By the way, use of the words "back in the day" refers to earlier times. When I hear this term, I think of the scripture John 9:4: "I must work the works of him that sent me, while it is day: the night cometh, when no man can work." This leads me to believe that the times we are presently living in must be night. Can we no longer work because night is here? I certainly do not want to believe that night is here. I would rather believe it is twilight, and we still have some daylight left to work the works of Him who sent us.

Along with pastors, assistant pastors, deacons, and lay members, the church also consisted of church mothers, who were highly respected and feared. If the church was large enough, there was a choir director, an organist, and a piano player. There were no drums, guitars, or electric organs back in the 1960s. People used washboards rubbed with twisted hangers, and they also used tambourines. Usually, there would be about five to ten separate families in one church. Everybody was not necessarily related to everyone else in the church, as is the case of some Pentecostal churches today.

On occasion, large numbers of black congregants in Harlem and other parts of New York City would attend special services en masse when famous evangelists came to town, like Reverend Billy Graham,

1

the late, great Reverend A. A. Allen, or the late, great Reverend R. W. Schambach—even though all three ministers were white. The local church members from most of the smaller churches would attend these big-time revival meetings, held under the big gospel tent, at Madison Square Garden in Manhattan or at Rockland Palace up in Harlem. In the case of Reverend Billy Graham, who filled stadiums, these were the mega-churches of the day.

I believe a few black ministers who had large audiences were the Reverend Frederick J. Eikerenkoetter II, better known as Reverend Ike, and Apostle Arturo Skinner, who headed the Deliverance Evangelistic Churches from the 1960s until his death in 1975.

What made me so anxious in 1971 to find carfare for the ride down to Madison Square Garden to see Reverend Ike was his advertisements over the gospel radio stations. I was a young teenager curious to hear this dynamic preacher who declared, "The *lack* of money is the root of evil," taking his slant of the verse found in 1 Timothy 6:10, "For the love of money is the root of all evil: which while some coveted after, they have erred from the faith, and pierced themselves through with many sorrows." Reverend Ike promised to tell us how to get rich. He promised to tell us his big secret of how we could have "our pie in the sky, now," instead of waiting for the hereafter.

We poor-working-our-way-off-the-welfare-waiting-for-a-blessing folks wanted to know Reverend Ike's secret. Reverend Ike was a millionaire, and he promised to share his secret of how we can get everything we needed or wanted, *now*. Needless to say, Madison Square Garden was packed! I was sitting way up in the nosebleed seats, following along with him in the Bible trying to unlock the secrets to riches. His secret? Put the largest sacrificial offering you have in your pocket into the bucket that was being passed around.

Later, the Reverend Fred C. Price was a black pastor who had a television program in the 1970s, and he simply taught from the Bible. On his televised program, no songs were sung, there were no splashy sets, and absolutely no gimmicks were used whatsoever. He came on television with the Bible in his hand and he just walked up and down the pulpit reading and teaching the Word. He kept your attention.

He was attractive, intelligent, and very true to form, a teacher of the Word. His church audiences were large and very attentive to every word that proceeded from his mouth. His television audiences looked very intellectual, well dressed, and, well, studious. I had never seen a black church that looked like this in all my young years.

My favorite television pastor, later on in my life, was the late, great Reverend G. E. Patterson. I loved to turn him on every Sunday morning and listen to him preach the unadulterated Word of God. He was definitely from the "former" church. He praised and worshipped the old-fashioned way. He was plainly spoken, but he was fueled with passion and anointing. His preaching voice was so anointed that he could take you from despair and sadness to happiness and hopefulness in one sermon. He was a "former" church preacher for "latter" church saints! He was an old-fashioned, down-home preacher!

Let me digress. In the black Pentecostal church, we love to hear the sound of a preacher's voice: his tones, yells, sighs, hollers, and hums. Not just Pentecostals, but Baptist and Methodist preachers hum and holler sermons too. I wonder if the apostle Paul had a voice people could listen to for a long time. I do not know. A story in the Bible told of a poor fellow who went to sleep during one of the apostle Paul's sermons and fell out of the window and died (Acts 20:9). The apostle prayed for him and brought him back to life.

Did Jesus ever hum a sermon? Where did that come from? There are quite a few ministers who can sing a sermon into the stratosphere. In the black church, ministers often sing and hum their sermons. Their melodious voices could move you to tears. One such preacher nowadays is Bishop Paul S. Morton of Louisiana. Oh my, how I can listen to him preach all day long! His melodic voice emphasizes the gospel in such a way that your faith increases and you just believe the victory is right around the corner.

Most congregants from the former church felt that if the preacher did not sing-song parts of his sermon and rear back and hold one ear, then he didn't preach. However, this kind of preaching is becoming a thing of the past. There are still a few preachers who sing sermons, but more and more Pentecostal preachers are standing behind glass lecterns and speaking professorially to the congregation. The movement of a firebrand preacher rearing back and holding an ear, with robes billowing as he moves, are few and far between.

One of the latest black Pentecostal ministers who could pack a convention center is the Reverend T. D. Jakes. In my opinion, I would call Bishop Jakes a former *and* latter church minister because he came up in the former church with its old-time testimony and song worship services. I also view him as a latter church minister because he is technologically advanced, holds worldwide conferences, seminars, and services, and heads up his own businesses outside the church as a published author and movie producer.

When I watch the television broadcasts of Bishop T. D. Jakes, or attend one of his services, I see at times he goes back to preaching the old-fashioned way, if the Spirit so moved him. But, most times, he speaks professorially and gives lectures on current topics, referencing Scripture. I suppose our Lord and Savior Jesus Christ and the apostles spoke more in this way.

Before Reverend Jakes became rich and famous, I remember watching him preach under Pastor Jasper Rolle's tent on 149th Street in the South Bronx. Bishop Jakes wasn't an exceptional preacher, nor did he stand out from any of the other dynamic preachers of that time. What made Bishop Jakes exceptional was a message he distributed on VHS tape titled "Woman Thou Art Loosed." This message was not hollered out; no rearing back, no hiccupping—it was a straight-at-you message to all the women in the church who felt trapped. The Reverend Jakes used the illustration of a woman giving birth. He illustrated how, through hard labor, she has to *push* her way out of her bondage. He stressed the need to push until you break forth into your deliverance. In all the years I have been sitting on the pews of the church, I do not remember a sermon where a male preacher, especially a male black preacher, told women they no longer needed to continue to suffer in silence under the iron thumbs of men.

Needless to say, Bishop Jakes's "Woman Thou Art Loosed" message made a few men of the church none too happy. Women who dared to think they could head up their own ministries and churches after listening to Bishop Jakes's message were called "loose women" by many men of the church. From that message, Bishop Jakes's ministry took off, and to this day his ministry and business acumen is par excellence.

Today, there are quite a few mega-churches all over the country. Some mega-churches came out of the Pentecostal Church; however, most do not use this denomination in their church's name. People attending these churches are not Pentecostal, Baptist, Methodist, or Episcopalian; they're just members of a "center." They use names like Christian Cultural Center, Life Christian Center, or Community Christian Center. With the nondenominational names, these mega-churches are able to incorporate all kinds of activities into their churches, which beforehand were never held in most Pentecostal churches. Calling the church a Christian Center releases it from rules, regulations, or restrictions that might be imposed from an organized denomination. This gives it freedom to host all kinds of entertainment, such as plays, movies, and concerts across the pulpit. So I ask again, is the church a place for entertainment and a community center? Or is it a place to pray, testify, worship, and listen to sermons across the sacred desk?

Let's consider and compare our old way of worship to how we worship today. We will consider if our worship is moving our faith forward or further away from the mark of the high calling of Christ Jesus our Lord. We Pentecostal Christians must discern if the ways in which we worship are fruitful and beneficial, or are they just bodily exercise that profits us little (1 Tim. 4:8).

People are certainly dying, I mean literally dying, for their freedom to worship God in the beauty of holiness all over the world. We must take worship seriously and appreciate the opportunity and freedom we have to do so. We must also sincerely seek the face of God to determine if we are worshipping in vain. Our worship should not be done solely to keep us entertained or to entertain the young people.

When the Spirit moves and falls over a service, the excitement comes, the exhilaration we feel is real, and the Glory of God fills the temple and our hearts and minds are changed for the better. We should dissect our songs, messages and praises in order to determine if they are right, if they are sincere. Is it pleasing to our God? Are we worshipping Him in true holiness? Are we doing what we do only to glorify flesh?

We members of the Pentecostal Church must live a life above reproach. We can only live a Saved and Sanctified life by being born again, born of the Spirit, which will give us the power to live according to the Word of God. We must be a light in this dark and evil world. Our first work and purpose is to reach souls to be Saved; then have those souls join the church. A person coming into the church from a world of sin should be led to the altar to pray the prayer of repentance.

Let me show the difference between sinners coming to the altar then and how they come now, as I view it from the pew. In the Scriptures, there is the story of a woman caught in the very act of adultery. St. John 8:10b-11 reads: *"Woman, where are those thine accusers? Hath no man condemned thee? She said, No man, Lord. And Jesus said unto her, Neither do I condemn thee: go, and sin no more."* After the Lord rescued her from the people who wanted to stone her to death, I sometimes wonder if she sinned again. I reasoned she continued to live a righteous life because it was Jesus Himself who rescued her. Because Jesus was sinless, she didn't find out later that the Man who saved her had hidden sins and shortcomings.

In the 'former' church, Saved, Sanctified, and Holy Ghost-filled members of the church generally were that, Saved! Not to put my trust in the arm of flesh, but back then, most of the converts were a light in a dark world and did set examples. Back then, there was more to the prayer for Salvation than just a slap on the forehead and altar ministers taking you to the back and giving you some pamphlets. I must say, from my own experience, you actually felt something. You actually witnessed people whose lives were changed. You could actually see burdens lifting; you saw people running, crying, skipping, and jumping around the altar as they received Salvation. You saw the change, and it lasted longer than a day!

After receiving Salvation, from my own experience, I felt like I could conquer the world! I felt I could actually live a life of righteousness for the rest of my life. As I paraphrase Psalms 18:29, I felt like I could run through troops and jump over walls. However, after going through a few trials and tribulations, the euphoria wore off. Days, and sometimes years, of discouragements, grief and sorrow come in life. Disappointments and pain come as time goes on. But my faith sustained me. As I continued to pray and learn the Scriptures, I persevered. Psalms 124:1 reads: *"If it had not been for the Lord who was on my side; Let Israel say. . . ."* I say, I know I would have given up a long time ago.

| CHAPTER 2 |

The Right Way to Worship

This topic, as a whole, is very serious and I hope it gives us pause to contemplate in our hearts if our praise and worship to Our Lord and Savior Jesus Christ is true. My personal feeling is that in order to worship, the sanctuary should be solemn and holy. All its furnishings, the pews, pulpit, communion table, vases, and instruments should be handled with care and prayer. I think the church should be kept clean and polished, free of rubbish, food, and chewing gum sticking to the bottom of the pews. We must adhere to the Word of God and stay completely true to it. With this in mind, I will touch on areas in the church where I think we may have strayed. I do believe, however, we can pray about it and reconsider and seek Our Lord and Savior Jesus Christ for guidance in these areas.

I think prayer should be convened before every service. The presence of God should be felt in the sanctuary as the souls approach the altar. The sanctuary does not have to be fancy, with crystal chandeliers hanging from the ceiling and gold wrapped around the altar. The church should be a place where the Spirit of the Lord can be felt, while also being inviting to the public. A lost soul should not be confused about where he is and why he's there. Therefore, a church should be respected also, and we should adhere to its rules and dress accordingly. This is my opinion.

Let me start by saying, I am not a theologian or a Bible scholar. I am not a preacher, pastor or hold any position of authority in the church. I have been a devotion leader on occasion and at times a Sunday school teacher. I was a member of a prayer band, consisting of a group of Pentecostal members visiting homes, hospitals, prisons, and nursing homes to pray for people. I am also a church administrator/secretary. I also have been an usher at times. All of this work does not make me an expert on Scripture nor does it make me an authority on church protocols or church worship. My interpretation of Scripture will be elementary at best, however, my writing on the subject of the Pentecostal faith stems from years of experience being a pew-viewer. This is the extent of my knowledge of the Pentecostal Church.

The hardest persecution I have experienced in my lifetime for being a Christian is very minor in comparison to the horrible persecution others have endured and are still enduring. As I mentioned before, as a child of the 1960s, my being a member of the Pentecostal faith caused me to be subjected to teasing and bullying by school children. Children called me names like 'Holy Roller' and 'church girl' while beating me up and chasing me home.

As a young adult in the 1970s and 1980s, I found people were more accepting of Pentecostals. More people were openly confessing to be 'born again' Christians, when before we were considered crazy people. Most of my experiences occurred in the black Pentecostal churches, therefore, my expertise, if you would call it that, will be from that viewpoint.

Nothing remains the same. After each passing year, even we ourselves have changed. Our towns and cities have changed; our lives have changed; our ways of communicating have changed. So, it is not surprising to see how much the church itself has changed. I do not expect today's Christians to walk around wearing robes and sandals, riding on donkeys and reading from scrolls. I love the fact that everything changes with time, but God never changes. His Word never changes. Hebrews 13:8 reads: *"Jesus Christ the same yesterday, and today, and forever."* Jesus said, in St. Matthew 22:37-39, *"Thou shalt love the Lord thy God with all thy heart, and with all thy soul, and with all thy mind. This is the first and great commandment. And the second is like unto it, Thou shalt love thy neighbor as thyself.*" This Scripture fits all generations and generations to come; it fits all forms of life, in all eras of time.

In the 'former' church, there was no time limit to a service. Often, we attended Sunday school, then morning worship service, then a young people worship service in the afternoon, called YPWW; then there was the evening service that could last until almost midnight. Compared to the 'latter' church of today, everything is rushed. In general, there is Sunday school for about an hour, now called the "School of Learning"; morning worship service, if more than two hours is unusual, and that includes the sermon. Because everything is rushed, and the entire service is timed, the outpouring of the Holy Spirit usually does not happen. There is the praise and worship portion, where the praise team sings all the songs; immediately after is the taking up of the offering; then words from the minister; a quick call for Salvation and then dismissal. If morning service starts at 11:00 a.m., you are out of there and on your way home before 2:00 p.m.

Some churches have two services; one in the morning at 8:00 a.m. that has to be out before 10:00 a.m. to prepare for the 11:00 a.m. people to start their service. These double services on Sundays started when some churches were too small to accommodate all its members in one service. This was never, ever heard of in the 'former' Pentecostal Church. To my remembrance, only the Catholic Church had hour-long masses several times on Sunday.

Let's discuss double services on Sundays. Is that progress? Rushing through one service in order to have another seems to cheat one of the two services. The pastor might receive a special anointing with his sermon in the morning, and then he is too drained to conduct the next service. Or the opposite might happen, the pastor may have less energy in the early service and be fully anointed and on fire in the second service.

I attended the second service of a big Pentecostal church down South (I won't say the city, because you might guess the church). While we stood in the foyer, waiting for the first service to end, people inside were in the midst of praising the Lord. The pastor was still in the pulpit preaching and the power was falling. We could hear the people in the sanctuary wailing in praise, while some danced before the Lord. We were not let into the main sanctuary because then the church would be overcrowded. However, I must say, inside the sanctuary there were plenty of empty seats.

By the time they emptied out the church to allow us to enter, our praise leader was decidedly colder. It was harder for people to get into the Spirit. When the pastor came back out, he had a towel around his shoulders and looked like he was ready to go lie down and rest. What was more disheartening, instead of a fiery, good message for us second-service participants, all the poor pastor could muster up was to tell us how the Lord really moved during the first service.

Some pastors stretch themselves really thin by opening churches in different sections of the same city. One pastor may have one church in two locations. Then another pastor has one church in three locations or even four locations. There's no time to meet and greet the people. The pastor does not participate in the praise and worship portion, which is very necessary to flow in the service. Just my view from the pew, I love a pastor that takes time to participate in Sunday school. When I see a pastor sitting in Sunday school, even participating in it by explaining some of the lessons in the Bible with the class, he or she adds more dimension to the class. If the pastor is ripping and running, he misses out on these special moments with his flock.

In the 1990s, I personally observed, very profoundly, that the way we worship changed. For five years, we would travel upstate to attend the annual holy convocation of a Pentecostal church. The holy convocation consisted of a few churches from up and down the eastern border of the country, including several attendees from the South, converging on this upstate church. I must say, the services were highly anointed and the messages that came across the pulpit were excellent. We made this our annual vacation destination to fellowship with like-minded members of the church for the week-long convocation. The church was packed with participants. There were baptisms done, christenings, weddings, even picnics between services. Bus loads would stop in for some of the services. The choir, which includes people from all of the visiting churches, sang the songs of Zion which lifted hearts and made everyone happy.

The presiding bishop is a man of great knowledge of the Bible, who is revered by many far and wide. This particular church was strict Pentecostal that didn't tolerate sin of any kind. People were prayed for and delivered from all manner of vices and sins. We, the participants, attended the morning prayers that began each day at six in the morning by someone starting to sing the song "Rise, Shine, Give God the Glory!"

It was common to see people slain on the floor under the Spirit, others joyfully crying out to the Lord, and someone running around the perimeters of the church. The atmosphere was charged with the presence of the Lord so heavy, I could even see white fog in the air in the church. Our souls were fed as well as our bodies. The church ladies cooked, cooked, cooked, feeding the attendees each and every night. We were even sent back to our hotels with small bags of snacks for the evening.

After five years of attending these powerful holy convocations, I began to notice attendance dwindling. Not only were the remaining attendees becoming discouraged, the bishop also became dismayed and spoke on people waxing cold in their walk with the Lord. By the late 1990s, after seeing the attendance dwindling by either the exodus of the young people or the death of older ones, the bishop decided to introduce something new at the last holy convocation I attended. Something called "The Paradigm Shift" was introduced. Around this time, everyone was talking about this 'paradigm shift' not only at this holy convocation, but in other churches I fellowshipped as well. Messages and prophesies came forth introducing this paradigm shift that will take the church in a new direction.

At my last attendance at this upstate convocation, the church was ninety percent empty. My friend who introduced me to this convocation had passed away a few months before. The bishop introduced a couple of ladies who stood in front of the church wearing pantsuits. I mention the pantsuits because women wearing pants was never before permitted in this particular church. So we were fixated on the pants the women were wearing while they introduced this new 'paradigm shift' that the church will undergo, which would erase all traditionalism. I sat in my seat thanking God my friend who introduced me to this convocation had now gone on to glory and could not see or hear this presentation.

The shift consisted of putting away the old rules and traditional ways of doing things in the church and embracing more progressive ideas. The women kept using the word 'traditional' as if the way things were traditionally done was wrong. Now the age of enlightenment has come, and this 'paradigm shift' will put the church on a more accurate and correct path. The new paradigm shift and the church can be researched on the Internet, revealing in more detail the changes it proposes and the way it seeks to break down the rules of the church. I can only write about how it affected me and the churches I attended in the 1990s.

This last holy convocation was very solemn and subdued. People were not praising and worshipping the Lord with all their might as before. The messages that came across the pulpit from the last remaining ministers were dry and dead. The choir members were gone, and more importantly the presence of the Lord was gone. I still have the printed program today in my files from this last convocation I attended. It reminds me of the end of church as we knew it. What also saddened me was the bishop's attitude; he looked defeated. I wonder if he thought bringing these women in, exalting the new paradigm shift, was the only way to save his church from extinction. I won't mention the bishop's name or the city he is from because he is a very prominent figure. He still preaches around the country and his knowledge of the Bible is exceptional. I believe he found out that introducing this new 'paradigm shift' into his church did not increase the membership. The Bible reads in 1 Timothy 4:1, *"Now the Spirit speaketh expressly, that in the latter times some shall depart from the faith, giving heed to seducing spirits, and doctrines of devils."*

| CHAPTER 3 |

Sing Unto the Lord a New Song

One of the most startling changes in our churches today has been the music. The songs of worship, the accompanying music, and the dances performed to the music, primarily, has been the one attribute that distinguished the Pentecostal faith from other faiths.

In the early days, when you passed by a Pentecostal church, you heard the big bass drum, someone scraping a clothes hanger across a washboard, tambourines tinkling, feet stomping, and hands clapping. Some people were fearful to walk into a Pentecostal church because they were not knowledgeable of the Pentecostal faith. They would warn their children, "Don't go into that 'Holy Roller' church; those people will put something on you." Overcoming the fear and apprehension, and out of curiosity, many times the music and dancing drew people in and many have found Salvation.

I wonder if there were certain types of music Jesus might have considered sinful. I would surmise that the music Salome was dancing to in her quest for the head of John the Baptist (St. Matthew 14:1-11) may have been frowned upon. Maybe the music played at the wedding of Cana was more acceptable (St. John 2:1-11). The music King David danced out of his clothes to while bringing home the Arc of the Covenant (2 Samuel 6:14) was probably very celebratory. Moses's sister, Miriam, sang a song of praise as she and the women danced when the children of Israel were delivered out of Egypt (Exodus 15:20-21). The daughter of Jephthah came out of the tent playing her tambourine and dancing for joy in celebration of her father's return (Judges 11:34). The music and dance episodes of the Bible emphasized either victory and praise or seduction and deceit. Both Miriam and Jephthah's daughter danced a 'praise' dance to the Lord.

The dancing Salome was doing would probably be considered sinful. Miriam and the women at the Red Sea were not dancing to solicit the desires of men, but were giving thanks and praises to God. This is where the Pentecostal faith anchored its hard and fast rule in the 'former' church against dancing.

Surely, there are different types of music for different events. Certainly, there are songs that have been inspired by God. People write or sing songs from experiences, derived from deep feelings stemming from various situations in life; their love for the opposite sex, their deep hatred of something, their love for their mother, or maybe their admiration of the environment. Also, songs come to people in different ways; in their sleep, while they are driving along or just inspiration. Therefore, some songs can be sinful and some songs can be songs of praise.

The Word of God says in Psalms 96:1, God can give a person a 'new' song. A song no one has ever heard before, in a tune never heard before. When this happens, these are special times and special songs. Some songs are borne out of pain, other songs out of happiness. I recall having dreams of singing the most beautiful song, the words and the melody so heavenly. The minute I awake, I forget the song. I wish I could have written it down, but no matter how hard I try to remember, the song is gone from my mind. There are those who are gifted in song writing; they can use a few words and create an entire song around those few words.

God created music, of course. The Bible states in Revelation 5:11, *"And I beheld, and I heard the voice of many angels round about the throne and the beasts and the elders: and the number of them was ten thousand times ten thousand, and thousands of thousands;"* Angels sing in Heaven, praising and worshipping God. Here on Earth, choirs, soloists and church members sing songs of praise worshipping God. I believe the angels in Heaven sing only praise songs to God. On Earth, there are people who sing only praise songs worshipping God. Then, there are some gospel singers who also sing other types of songs. From reading the Bible verse above, we learn the angels sing songs of praise and worship God. So, what am I saying? Should we only sing songs of praise, worshipping God?

This has been the dilemma for gospel singers for years. God has given some people the gift to sing, voices that will melt your heart. In the 'former' church, great, great gospel singers came out of the church and made it big singing secular songs. Back in the 'former' church, they could not readily call themselves gospel singers if they were also singing secular songs. On the other hand, there are secular singers who can sing gospel songs better than any gospel singer. However, they will always be considered secular singers by the Pentecostal Church because they sing other types of songs. More recently, great gospel singers have come out of the Pentecostal Church. I can understand the tension when a gospel artist wants to sing secular songs; however, the Pentecostal Church was not having it. You are either in the church all the way, or out.

From reading autobiographies and biographies of some of these singing artists, I know of their love of gospel music, and their love for the Lord, but the fame and fortune pulled them further away from the church and its teachings. No one wants to wallow in poverty when you have the voice to sing and the opportunity to make millions of dollars. So, a gifted gospel singer has to make a decision. Will I use my gift solely to reach souls for Christ, or will I use it to also benefit myself and my family? Can I reach more souls for Christ if I sing outside the church? Should I write my songs and music to be more appealing to the world at large, or will the world pull me away from the church?

The Bible does say in Proverbs 18:16, *"A man's gift maketh room for him, and bringeth him before great men."* Many people wrongly used this verse of Scripture to charge fees or honorariums to sing a song in a service, play an instrument or direct a choir. A gifted gospel singer, with a voice that could crack crystal, is sought after by big record companies and movie studios. Some of these singers earn large amounts of money and some have branched out into other fields without leaving the church. However, if they are singing songs other than gospel songs, they are not considered gospel singers by the Pentecostal Church.

In recent times, we see rappers who have given up their secular careers and joined the church. They were famous and at times prosperous singing their hits and entertaining thousands of people. They felt emptiness in their heart and wanted more from life and decided to come to the church to find answers. On the other hand, we see gospel artists that have left the church to sing popular songs. They were once prominent gospel singers, reaching many people with their songs; now they want to be accepted by the world and recognized as a pop artist. They decided the opportunity to succeed is more readily available singing pop songs than singing even their contemporary gospel songs. Sadly, their hearts are hurting with despair and loss.

The secular artists who gave up all to follow Jesus had to reconcile in their minds that they might not receive all the adulation and riches they once knew as a secular artist. They are alright with that because what they are receiving in return is peace of mind, truth and sound relationships with their spouse and family. I know of a couple of artists, once successful in the secular world, now content with running a church and singing only gospel songs. They were ready to give up the world and to follow Jesus. Just like the rich, young ruler who had to sell all his riches and follow Jesus. You will be blessed in a more perfect way.

The drawback is many gospel singers compare the money famous pop singers demand and they want to reach that level. The pop singers are filling stadiums, arenas and large venues all over the world. When the pop stars land at airports, there are throngs of people waiting for them. The pop stars have security details protecting them as ecstatic fans run behind the artists' limousines. People pay hundreds, even thousands of dollars for a ticket to see these pop stars. Promoters and record companies foot the bill for travel, food, hotels, cars, etc. Gospel singers want the same adulation and star treatment, so their contracts require expensive suites at four-star hotels, fees with astronomical, high-end amenities. Because they do not draw the size of crowds that can meet all these requirements, they feel slighted. Not only are there no throngs of fans to meet them at the airport, they must go to the baggage claim and pick up their own bags, and sometimes have to flag down a taxi to take them to the venue. Most often, the venue is a church with a couple hundred people waiting, who paid about twenty-five dollars to see them.

Gospel artists view the Grammy, the Stellar or the Dove Awards as the epitome of success of their worth and accomplishments. When some gospel singers are awarded a Stellar or a Dove Award, they believe their fees should be higher, and in raising their price they then priced themselves out of a job. From my view from the pew, I've seen gospel singers who are at a much lower level of fame and fortune, nowhere near the level of super pop stardom, who demand higher pay.

My mother and I have attended numerous Stellar Awards in New York City and in Nashville, Tennessee before the awards moved to Las Vegas. We once attended a Grammy Awards ceremony in Los Angeles, California. At the Grammy Awards, the gospel segment was a small, small portion of the show. Although the Stellar Awards celebrates and awards all gospel artists, they seem to center around the same five or six top gospel artists every year. I know there are so many gospel singers in the country who are never recognized or awarded for their many years of singing gospel songs. These gospel artists are scratching their way up the ladder trying to gain some form of recognition.

Winning a Stellar Award or maybe even a Grammy, the newly awarded gospel artists feel justified in charging gospel promoters exorbitant performance fees. Maybe a mega-church could afford to pay their price, but the average church wanting to hold a gospel program to raise money for a new roof can't afford them. I have seen the gospel artists who cannot receive their asking price go to the media and ridicule the church and all Christians for not supporting gospel music. They fail to realize that people who are NOT true born again Christians, will not pay large sums of money to hear songs about giving up worldly pleasures and sins.

Gospel artists, I hate to say, do not have the fan base like the pop commercial artists. I always say this and this is what I believe: *Gospel songs, no matter how much they are jazzed up, will never be _popular_ because the songs require the hearer to make a decision.* Other songs may inspire, at times, or even move the listener to do better in their lives, but the listener can take it or leave it. In most new inspirational songs, most of the time, the lyrics do not encourage soul searching to decide to follow Our Lord and Savior Jesus Christ, as it would have done in an old-time gospel song.

What is peculiar to me is noticing how many very well-known secular artists, who had big major hit records back in the day, now turn to gospel after their record sales dried up. What usually occurs is the gospel songs they now sing are in the same vein as their secular hits. I love those old secular artists and I'm glad they found the Lord before it was too late. A few secular artists have come over to gospel and now record only gospel songs. I understand they have to sing in their own individual styles, but at times the beat and rhythm simply do not fit in a church service.

Not placing him in the same vein as an artist who came up in a Pentecostal church, I was really surprised to learn how much Elvis Presley loved and recorded gospel. I would place him in the category of people who can sing gospel songs better than any gospel artist, without being a gospel artist.

There are two gospel albums by secular artists I think are really sincere and respectful of the church and Our Lord and Savior Jesus Christ. The first is Aretha Franklin's *Amazing Grace* album. Every song on that album is an old traditional gospel song enveloped in the gifted voice of The Queen of Soul. The other album was recorded by the late, great secular artist Bobby Womack. His album, *Back to My Roots*, is another all-time great gospel album. In my opinion, each song Mr. Womack performed on this album was done with deep conviction on his part and a sense of spirituality and pain. You could feel his soul crying out for Salvation, especially on the cut "It Is Well." His rendition of that song sent electricity up and down my spine. He was crying out on that song from all the pain he went through in his life. He and his brothers started out singing only gospel.

Bobby Womack said his father cried when he and his brothers went over to secular music. The Bible says in Mark 8:36, *"For what shall it profit a man, if he shall gain the whole world, and lose his own soul?"* Bobby Womack's answer after a lifetime of crisis, drug abuse, marital upheavals, and the untimely deaths of a couple of his brothers and two of his children—"Nothing!" Both these artists were raised in the church and know how to sing gospel songs with feeling. However, after recording these great gospel albums, they went back to singing their secular hits as before.

For sure, back in the day, a gospel artist could not record a purely secular album and then come back and record a gospel album without much ridicule from the church. The situation is a little different for the Queen of Soul, I believe. She came out of the Baptist Church, which I believe is not as strict as the Pentecostal faith. She could sing her "Rock Steady" song on stage and no one would dream of stopping her from walking up to a pulpit in *any* church to sing "Amazing Grace." Her God-given voice is just *made* for the church.

Singing only gospel is not only the rule of the Pentecostal Church, but the conviction of its singers. If you are a confessed, Saved, and Sanctified Christian in the Pentecostal Church, a person sold out to the Lord to reach souls, you do not want to sing secular songs. Your desire is to use your gift for the uplifting of the kingdom and to reach souls. A very close relative once asked me, "Is it fair that secular artists can become gospel artists, after years of people bumping and grinding to their hits?" (That's if you believe it is wrong to dance to secular music as the old Pentecostals believe.) After thinking about it for a while, my answer is, "Yes!" Yes, it is fair because I believe that a secular artist can repent and become a gospel artist after Salvation. Look at Apostle Paul who had many Christian men, women and children persecuted before he found the Lord. All his prior dealings with Christians were forgiven when he accepted Jesus Christ and began to preach the Gospel. Although Paul had to suffer for the Gospel, he was forgiven.

Many famous and successful R&B and hip hop artists have revealed they were raised in the holiness church as children. To the amazement of us all, some of the most 'out there' people were raised in the church. They began chasing after fortune and fame, which caused most of them great grief later in their lives. Some of them made it back to the church before they were totally destroyed, while others did not. The ravages of living a sinful and ungodly life took its toll on their minds and bodies. Some of them look much older than their years; others had everything and lost everything. Their foundation in the holiness church spared some of them from total despair. They remembered some of the church teachings and sought the Lord for help in their time of need. The Bible says in Proverbs 22:6, *"Train up a child in the way he should go: and when he is old, he will not depart from it."*

When the great gospel group the Winans transitioned to become more commercial, which appeared to me, unnatural for them, I remember watching them sing on the television show *Soul Train*. The Winans appeared to me to be very uncomfortable singing their hit song "Don't Leave Me" on television. After years of hearing the Winans sing songs like "Millions," "Tomorrow" and "Restoration," watching them try to move to the beat of their new hit "Don't Leave Me" on *Soul Train* was strange. Even Don Cornelius asked them what they were trying to do. Their reply was to reach the young people for Jesus. I hope this moved the young people to turn their lives around and receive Salvation after that performance. Looking at the expressions on the Winans's faces as the young people swayed and waved their arms before them on *Soul Train*, I think I knew what was on their minds. I believe they were thinking: "We do not want these people to start dancing to our song on national television because in the Pentecostal Church, it is a sin to do worldly dances." I believe they were conflicted.

Personally, I love the Winans. I raised my children on all their albums. Back in the 1980s, I rented a van and took all my friends to a college out in New Jersey to see them and the Williams Brothers perform. I always liked to share any happiness I have with people I am close to. So, I rented a van and filled it up with family and friends to go to the concert that night. I wanted them to see the Winans in person! In the middle of the concert, Marvin Winans walked out into the audience and shook hands with the elated fans, and one of them was mine! I thought I would never wash my right hand again! We had a glorious time.

At times, even the worldly sinner seemed to give more respect to a gospel song and refrained from dancing when they knew the performer was a gospel artist. This is where the 'former' church and the 'latter' church clash. Are we winning souls to Salvation, or are we winning Grammy, Stellar or Dove awards, accolades, fortune, fans, and fame? Is the church too closed up, needing to open up more and reach out to the world at large by encouraging its singers to go on more secular shows and dance shows? If the church holds to its standards, will it discourage the young people from reaching out into questionable venues? Mark 16:15 reads: *"Go ye into all the world, and preach the gospel to every creature."* All the world means everywhere. We should go into all the world and share the Gospel, but we should not do what they are doing as we go out. Just my view.

An example of what I mean, when I say we should not do what they do as we share the Gospel, consider gospel singers who are well known for several gospel hit songs, bringing untold thousands of souls into the church; then, the people see the gospel artist performing the latest dances to their songs. This reduces the gospel songs to pop songs, taking away the spirituality of the songs. By dancing the latest dance craze while singing the gospel song often takes away the sacredness of the song. It also takes away the anointing on the gospel singer who performs the song. Instead of growing in the ministry, the gospel artist languishes in indecision and confusion.

Incorporating new, more popular upbeat songs into the church was a slow, gradual infiltration. For example, say your choir decides to sing a very, very contemporary gospel song from one of the gospel artists of the day. In order for the choir to sing this song, the choir would have to move to the beat of the song. The musicians are moving to the rhythm of the song along with the congregation. More and more songs in this vein come in and then the robes come off, and before you know it people are rocking out the latest dance moves in the church.

Around the 1990s, pastors began screening songs the choirs wanted to sing. In the 'former' church, the choir stood up, announced the number of the hymnal song they would be singing, and everyone sang along. In the fire-baptized holiness church, the choir would sing one of their haphazard songs like "What's the Matter with Jesus, He's Alright," and everyone joined in. In the 'latter' church, the pastor now has to conference with the choir director to see if the song they want to sing is suitable.

I remember an incident during the services at one of the Pentecostal churches I attended, where instead of the choir marching down the aisle two-by-two, looking straight ahead, singing "We're Marching to Zion," the choir marched down the aisle doing three steps forward, two steps back, a turn to the right, and a turn to the left, all the way down the aisle, singing Kirk Franklin's "Melodies from Heaven." The music was slamming (as they say) and the beat to the song was rocking. This was all new to the old Pentecostal way of worship. I believe the pastor saw the choir's movements with the music was glorifying the flesh more than praising and worshipping God, and the march was discontinued.

There are some gospel artists whose primary goal is *not* to sing to save souls or to minister. Their main purpose for singing is to win those awards, and to become rich and famous. While they have the gift to sing and were gifted from a young age, they just happened to sing gospel because their mothers might have put them up in front of a church when they were young. It was never their intention to become just gospel singers, or to reach souls for Salvation. As these singers grew older, they left the church and secured profitable careers singing in other genres. A few of our edgy gospel artists are confusing to their fans, and certainly to the church. When you see them on television, they look and sound like the world. When I say 'world,' I mean their demeanor and persona are very, very contemporary.

A few years ago, I went to see an artist, whom I will not name here, whose records were really 'contemporary' gospel. I say really, really contemporary because if you listen to the song long enough, it can move from 'contemporary' over to 'temporary' gospel. The song may start off talking about Jesus, without mentioning His name of course, but by the end of the song, you begin to wonder. However, when I saw this artist at a church convention, the artist was super spiritual and very serious about reaching souls for Christ. The artist ridiculed anyone in the audience who stood and rocked to the songs. The artist said, "It's not about the beat to the songs, it's about getting serious about your soul salvation." The artist went on to sing traditional gospel songs, not the hits, and preached about where the audience will spend eternity. The audience was left confused and disappointed because they wanted to rock out to the artist's hit songs. Instead, they were told to consider their souls. Then it occurred to me, this was the artist's way of getting souls to the altar. Put out hit records with the right beat where the world would hear it, and then when the world comes to the concerts, preach to them the way of the cross.

As recognition, fame and fortune come to young gospel artists today, the enemy of our souls is pulling them away from the church and convincing them there is nothing wrong with singing secular popular songs. If a gospel singer's main reason for singing is to reach souls for Salvation, singing other songs professionally leaves them in a strange place. Some have said, "Oh, I can sing a love song to my spouse." Yeah, but is everyone else singing your love song to *their* spouse? Or will they sing your love song to someone else's spouse? On the other hand, if you are singing about Jesus and the fact that He died so that your soul won't be lost, then you can sing that to everybody. Your love song to your savior won't be turned into a lust song used to commit sin.

Love songs, recording love songs or gaining fame and fortune singing love songs that suggest committing fornication and adultery does not turn a sinful heart toward God. Some people may say, "But God is love, so I'm singing about love." Taking the name of Jesus out of the lyrics and replacing it with the word 'love' allows the gospel singer to ride the fence. They can sell more records, book more gigs, and reach a wider audience if they replace the name Jesus with 'love.' What's wrong with that? God is a jealous god and He does not need you to be lukewarm. He rather you be hot or cold. The Bible says if you are lukewarm, the Lord will spew you out of His mouth (Revelation 3:16). Also, if the songs are hard to discern and are confusing to potential souls because it sounds like the songs that can be heard at the bar, then the gospel singer defeats the purpose. Then again, it might reveal more about the singer himself. The singer's heart may be longing for that genre of songs and living that kind of lifestyle. Perhaps he needs to pray and ask the Lord to make his heart clean.

When the Clark Sisters came out with the song "You Brought the Sunshine," their song was played everywhere, even in the bars. The song itself didn't sound like one heard in any Pentecostal church. People outside the church were rocking and moving to the beat of the song until about the middle of the song you heard the name Jesus. Hearing the name Jesus made them stop and wonder, "Is this a church song?"

Songs can be positive and have the Salvation message in it, but will it be accepted in the church? Even the people at the bar stopped dancing to it. Hopefully, some souls were Saved after listening to "You Brought the Sunshine" who otherwise would have not heard it in a church. In that case, singing contemporary gospel may be a viable avenue to take, if it does not take the artists with it.

Money, trinkets, jewelry, cars, and material things motivate some gifted gospel singers to ride the fence. Most people of the 'former' church believe that if you are a gospel singer, you should only sing church songs. If a song causes you to think lustful, sinful thoughts, or even evil and dark thoughts, it should not be sung in the sanctuary. That goes for dance moves, too. If you are bumping and grinding, shaking and binding, those worldly dance moves do not belong in the sanctuary.

I wrote in my second book, *Screen Door: A Memoir*, about growing up in the Pentecostal faith where we were not allowed to listen to any other type of music but 'church' music. It's like growing up eating only cabbage and collard greens, only to find out as an adult you love broccoli, too. I realize I had missed out on years of songs that might have enriched my life. We called all other music 'devil music'; and back then, we turned the radio or television off as soon as those songs were played. I find I like gospel songs, and I also like soothing contemporary songs like "Bridge Over Troubled Water" and "I Believe In You and Me," songs performed by secular artists.

We found ourselves so set apart from important life events because of our upbringing in the Pentecostal faith. Because we did not dance or sing songs that were not gospel, we were not invited to too many family events like wedding receptions, birthdays or holiday parties. Fathers did not dance with their daughters at weddings. At the wedding reception, we did not have dances going on. No father-daughter dance, no groom-mother dance. Although, I did see on a recent YouTube video a father and daughter doing a church dance at a church wedding reception, which was strange to see. Would he have been so wrong if he danced with his daughter at the wedding? If we sang a secular song at someone's birthday party, would we miss Heaven? Those questions are for each one of us to search our own hearts about. But here is my own personal opinion—all music is not devil music, however, all types of music should not be played in our churches or in our hearts. Keep the church holy; keep the church sacred. Keep your hearts and minds pure. This is just my view from the pew.

Over the years, the music has certainly changed in the church. In addition to traditional gospel, there is jazz gospel, urban gospel, hip hop gospel, rap gospel, contemporary gospel, and one new to me called root gospel. Back in the 'former' church, Pentecostal churches sang all traditional gospel songs. If a choir sang a contemporary gospel song in the church, they were rebuked. As depicted in the movie, *Say Amen, Somebody*, the late, great gospel legend Thomas Dorsey endured much ridicule for bringing his style of gospel music into the church. His music was rejected because it sounded too much 'like the world.' Now his songs, such as "Precious Lord," are an old staple in the church and are considered 'traditional' compared to newer songs that came years later like, Edwin Hawkins's "Oh Happy Day."

In 1969, when "Oh Happy Day" hit the airwaves, most Pentecostal church leaders demanded their choirs not sing that song. It had a beat to it that made people want to dance. This song changed gospel music forever. The song was on the top ten and on all the radio stations, both religious and secular. The church did not know what to make of it. From my view from the pew, I would say "Oh Happy Day" opened the floodgates for all the contemporary songs that came after. The song encouraged people to really listen to the lyrics of a song in order to discern if the song was gospel or not. In the 'former' days, a gospel song was immediately recognized, but after "Oh Happy Day" that was no longer the case.

Years before, secular singers, who came out of the church, used to take gospel songs and change the lyrics for the worldly audience. They would be ridiculed by the same audiences they were trying to entice. The people outside of the church disapproved of singers bringing church songs into the clubs and bars. Even the sinners have respect for church music.

When it comes to our worship services, everything has turned around. The church moved from Sanctified, set aside and holy in their music and songs, to become more contemporary, common and casual. So much so, early one Sunday morning I had to wonder if I stepped into a church or a club. I'm serious! Inside this church, the ceilings were covered in drapes of cloths, the walls were also covered in different colored sheets, and the congregation was dancing to a popular hit secular song. The audience was not chanting "Hallelujah" or "Thank you, Jesus"; instead, they were chanting—I'll use a child's name—"Go, Tommy! Go, Tommy!" as a child danced in the front of the church. Is this the new way of worshipping Our Lord and Savior Jesus Christ? Since I was shocked and appalled at this show in the sanctuary, people may have felt I was judging. I'll just say, walking into that church expecting to see a worship service in progress, where people lift up holy hands to a holy God, instead I found a dance hall; so, yes, I did judge. In the 'latter' church, new converts come in unwilling to change or obey any rules of the church they do not agree with.

Being an older, seasoned pew-viewer, I should have stood up, like the Apostle Paul would have done, and proclaimed in indignation, "This is the House of God, not a club! This is NOT the way we worship the Lord! Now, turn on the lights and everyone run to the altar and ask for forgiveness!" Did I do that? No, I did not. What did I do? I did what most pew-viewers have done for years . . . nothing! I just sat there and looked like I just swallowed a bone.

Like most pew-viewers, I did not want to sow discord. I did not want people to not like me. I did not want to be the one who discourages the young people and causes them to leave the church. People have suggested to let the young people praise the Lord in their own way. If a child wants to do the 'running man' across the front of the sanctuary,

27

while the congregation chants "Go Tommy! Go Tommy!", then let him. Times have changed. The old traditional ways are no longer relevant. The young congregants—not all—are bringing worldly songs into the church. What is so alarming, the older congregants do not know the latest dances or songs anyway. So when the praise dancers are performing the 'Harlem Shake' during devotional service, the older congregants are not aware it is a worldly dance, but the young people are very much aware.

In the 'latter' church, the choir has to rock! They have to dance together, bump together, stomp together, clap up, clap down, and clap to the side. Some choirs are even doing worldly dance steps. There are choir directors doing theatrics; kicking, sliding and bouncing, everything but direct the choir. Some choir are not wearing robes, so you see very tight fitting dresses high above the knees and cut low showing cleavage. Some of the women are heavy set and very well endowed, so tight revealing dresses do not place people's minds heavenward. Very fancy hairdos, some heads shaved at the sides while the top is spiked up and carved out like the crown of birds; other hairstyles very long in all different colors. Even the men sport varying hairstyles and wear tight fitting clothes. Also, some choir members wear big jangling earrings and men wear diamond studs, make the choir look more like an entertainment troupe rather than a church choir.

During the choir performance, they move and rock to the songs by doing dances and claps to assimilate with the secular performers. At times, attempts at moving and dancing in sync takes away their ability to sing because some of them get out of breath. While there are songs that can be enhanced and emphasized, like maybe the tenors sing a part that is raised up, then combine that with the altos and sopranos in order to make the song sound more beautiful and harmonious; some of the new songs are enhanced so much that it sounds like, well, noise; and I don't mean a joyful noise.

Are the angels in Heaven doing acrobatics during their songs of praise to our Father which is in Heaven? Are they sliding, jumping, jerking, twerking, snapping fingers, and skipping around the throne of God? I wonder.

Oh, another thing, in the 'former' church you never, ever snapped your fingers to a gospel song. That's a 'former' church thing, you wouldn't understand. (I'd like to make tee shirts with this mantra on it: "It's A Former Church Thing!") When a person is standing on stage snapping fingers while singing a gospel song, a 'former' church member somewhere knows immediately that that person did not have good 'church training.'

Choir members and directors should ask themselves, is the song they sing reaching souls? Is the song helping someone in the congregation receive Salvation; or is their singing just putting on a show and entertaining the audience? Let's discuss, Church. Should choirs wear choir robes again? How we dress and what we wear on our bodies is still important, don't you think?

There is an old 1970s hip hop song that goes, "Throw your hands in the air and wave them like you just don't care." The 'latter' church chants it now and responds in kind, "Oh yeah; oh yeah." For another secular song titled "Ain't No Party," the lyrics were changed from 'West Coast' to 'Holy Ghost.' This catchy phrase that was a big hit for the rapper Coolio, back in the 1990s, can be heard at many church programs today. Congregants chant, "Ain't no party like a Holy Ghost party, 'cause a Holy Ghost party don't stop." Outside the church, this historic line is sung at so many parties and clubs with fill-in words to fit various occasions. Coming from the old church, using this phrase in a church makes no sense to me. Why are we having a party during a church service? In addition, from years of attending Bible study, I am always leery of using the words 'Holy Ghost' frivolously. The song sounds so carnal to me, but that's just my view from the pew.

There are other songs, phrases and terms that were taken from the streets and incorporated into worship services. There were occasions where a minister might slip up, or even purposely used slang or curse words during their sermons. Many young people, and I should add older people, do not want to be set aside, Sanctified and different from the world. On the contrary, they want to be just like everybody else and will do any- and everything the outside world does. There's no harm in it. Why not?

In many cultures in Africa, South America and Central America, the people perform the same celebratory dances outside of their churches as they do inside their churches. The difference is when the Holy Spirit moves them to dance, the dance will not be like any carnal dance done outside of the Spirit.

The Scripture from the beginning of this book asks, "Who can remember the church in her first glory?" I can! In the 'former' church, songs were inspired by the Holy Spirit. People sang from their experiences and from their prayer life. The songs came from within. The Pentecostal Church was known for even making up songs that had meaning only to them. In most of the small storefront Pentecostal churches, there were very few hymnals in the pews. In fact, hymnals were very rarely used. On many occasions, the church members only sang the chorus and not the verses. I was well into adulthood before finding out there were verses to most of the songs I sang in our worship services.

Here in the 'latter' church, a new form of dancing has presented itself into the church called 'Praise Dancing.' A group or troupe of dancers performs synchronized dancing usually to a gospel song played from the Internet, while the congregation looks on. Some of the dancing apparel may resemble that worn in the Bible days, like flowing dresses with tights or pants worn underneath and flowing scarves. Sometimes the dancers in the black churches wore white face or white masks. Why? I do not know. So, what's wrong with Praise Dancing? Nothing. However, compared to the 'former' church *everyone* danced in the Spirit. I ask, "Where is your praise?" Are we praising the Lord by sitting and watching others dance? Should we just throw on Yolanda Adams's or CeCe Winans's CD and let the praise dancers dance for us? Or is it still permissible for us to sing a song together and dance, if the Spirit so moves us?

Most recently I've been sitting in a Pentecostal church where no one had the opportunity to do anything during the service, unless you are called upon to say 'Amen.' No one just arbitrarily sang a song or testified during devotion. The praise leaders did all the singing; we, the congregants, just sang along. The praise dancers did all the dancing and, of course, the preacher preached. The congregation's non-participation would be understandable if we were a mega-church where it would be impossible for everyone to sing their own song. But we are sitting in a storefront, black Pentecostal church with less than twenty people in it, and that's including children!

The congregation, in the 'latter' church, now reads the lyrics of the song off a wall from a projector, while we try and keep up with the melody with the praise leader. Of course, we are not going to know every song, every time, but if the congregation is not with you, maybe you should incorporate a song everybody knows. If you are in a small storefront Pentecostal church, with no projector, you just listen to the song until you catch on. In the new 'latter' church, you can't sing your song, you can't dance your dance and, to add insult to injury, you can't even testify anymore!

Another distressing occurrence came up in the larger churches. Believe it or not, some praise leaders are hired by the church to 'conduct' worship and praise. These people are not necessarily members of the church; they have made careers out of being professional devotion leaders. They go from church to church conducting worship services before the pastor takes the podium to preach. When I heard this, I had to stand up from my view from the pew and shake my head in dismay. If I was pastoring this church, I would question what am I doing wrong that my members cannot sing songs of Zion and conduct worship services that I have to hire professional praise teams to come into my church?

OK, while I'm 'wiling out' (that is how young people describe when people overreact), I will add right here one thing that really irritates me to no end; that is a devotion leader who cannot sense the moving of the Spirit. When a devotion leader stands before an audience, one has to first sense the feeling of the audience, to find out if the people are excited to be there, or are tired or bored. The praise leader has to determine the mood of the congregation and choose songs that will uplift, comfort, encourage, or console the people. Let me explain why this is so important for those who have never sat in a real anointed devotion service. There are times during devotion when the praise leader may sing a song that will cause people to come out of a deep funk and revive them. The audience may then begin to praise the Lord right in the middle of the song, and the Spirit lifts their hearts out of despair. The congregation will go forth in a praise saying "Hallelujah" or "Thank you, Jesus." Some people in the congregation might stand and lift their hands in praise or move from their seats and break forth in dance. You may even see some people with their eyes closed, tears streaming down their cheeks and meeting under their chin. If devotion leaders are insensitive to the moving of the Spirit, they will hinder the movement of God in a service, thus, blocking people from getting blessed.

A bossy, controlling devotion leader who stops everything and directs people when to dance or when to praise the Lord is terrible. While the service is high and people are out of their seats in praise, and the musicians come in with the first down beat, nothing is more disparaging than when the devotion leader stops the music while people are dancing and praising the Lord. There are a few controlling ministers that will stop the music and ask the ushers to sit people down while they are still dancing in the Spirit. The congregation stops singing and looks up at the controlling devotion leader or minister, who only stops everything in order to control and then instruct the congregation to turn to their neighbor and say, "I don't know what you came to do, but I came to praise the Lord!" By this time, the Spirit had lifted from the service. Then the controlling devotion leader or minister instructs the congregation to speak in their spiritual tongues or dance and praise the Lord. Now the people are no longer in the Spirit and the atmosphere is cold. A sensitive, spirit-filled devotion leader or minister will know the moving of the Spirit and knows when the Spirit of God is moving in a service. Some of the 'latter' church ministers will feel the moving of the Spirit and say something like, "It's time for a praise-break right here!" The church then goes up in such a praise you feel like you could fly away right then and there! Hey, praise Him!!

I can remember when someone told a testimony and it moved people to see things in a whole new light. This testimony motivated people to make a change in their own life, or gave them new insight on a situation. A testimony can renew faith in difficult circumstances, and a person who had given up hope could begin to pray for the Lord to intervene in their situation. A testimony is a praise report. It tells of how or when the Lord healed someone physically or mentally. It tells of how or when the Lord supernaturally supplied a want or need. A testimony uplifts, renews, restores, and gives hope. The Bible reads in Revelation 12:11, *"And they overcame him by the blood of the Lamb, and by the word of their testimony; and they loved not their lives unto the death."*

During the devotion part of the service, a person may testify by giving thanks for whatever the situation may have been where the Lord provided in their life. Some people are highly emotional during testimony because the victory over the circumstance was so great; while other testimonies may be a little more subdued.

Most of the 'latter' churches have discontinued testimonies in worship services because many people do not know how to testify. Back in the old days, people spoke at the level of their intelligence. Some were good speakers, others were not. In the early churches, especially in the neighborhoods we lived in, the seniors testified speaking in bad English, telling of their trials and tribulations in their own way. Everyone understood what they meant to say, even though they said it wrong.

Then there is the person that likes to talk. Usually the testimony begins by giving honor to the pastor, the assistant pastor, the mother of the church, the elders, the deacons, the missionaries, the ushers, all the members of the church, and always ended with 'and even down to the little children,' before beginning their testimony. To add a little levity to this, I will tell a funny story to emphasize the testimony dilemma in the church. I do not like to tell jokes because some jokes can be lies, and I do not wish to lie in this book. But by telling this little funny story, you will be able to see the dilemma the church faced with testimonies:

> *A man visiting a church acknowledges the important people of the church body before testifying: "Before I testify, I would like to give honor to Pastor Dam, and his lovely wife, First Lady Dam, and I would also like to acknowledge his mother, Mother Dam, and her husband*

> *Deacon Dam. Matter of fact, I would like to give honor*
> *to the whole Dam family—and all the Dam children!"*

Okay, no more jokes. I promise.

When the church was in its first glory, the worship songs during testimony service praised God. Let's say someone starts the song "Glory, Glory, Hallelujah, Since I've Laid My Burden Down." After a couple stanzas, the person leading the song may testify about a burden they were carrying, and how the Lord answered prayer and now they can lay that burden down.

Or maybe the entire congregation may sing "What a Friend We Have in Jesus," and then go into prayer. People sang songs that were in their hearts, songs that may have dropped into their spirits helping others through some rough times. That was back in the days when the church was in its first glory, the 'former' days.

Now here we are in the 'latter' days, and the testimony part of the service has been done away with because, instead of people focusing on what the Lord had recently done in their lives, they ramble on about everything else. Some use this opportunity to bring up strife with someone else in the church, or talk about personal issues that's not appropriate for church service. Some people even start preaching during their testimony. Thus, testimonies have been discontinued. Should it remain so? Let's discuss.

In the 'former' days, you might walk into a Pentecostal church service and hear a gospel song like "Victory, Victory Shall Be Mine." The tambourines are going, the drums playing, the organ and piano holding the melodies, people swaying from side to side with their eyes closed, and the spirit of comfort filling the church. Someone may cry and raise their arms up in the air, praising God, feeling the Spirit of the Lord. This was the glory of the Pentecostal Church. This was when deliverance, freedom and victory came forth in the lives of many people. This was when a song gave praise to God because many of these songs were made up on the spot. Words were added to articulate what really happened in the lives of people. For example, the song "Victory, Victory Shall Be Mine," someone will change the lyrics and sing, "Joy, joy shall be mine" or "Peace, peace shall be mine." People were not always literate, educated or sophisticated, and the lyrics were not always proper, but it ministered to the hearts of the people.

Now, what I'm about to say, I hope will not offend anyone. Hear me out. I just want to show how jarring it was for me, an individual from the 'former' church in its first glory, when I walked into a new-style 'latter' church. I am just expressing this experience only to show a comparison.

Usually, a Pentecostal church is the noisiest church on the block. The music is blaring, the lights are on; there is loud singing, people dancing, hands raised in the air—very exciting and exhilarating. One Easter Sunday morning in Newark, New Jersey, back in the early 1990s, I experienced the church culture shock of my life. I visited a Pentecostal church and, for the first time, I saw a change in the way the worship service was conducted. The lights were off, and I could barely make out the silhouettes of people standing facing a wall. The song was one of those new songs, probably, "You Can Make It," a song by Tammy Faye Bakker from the new *700 Club* TV show. This song encourages people when they are going through adversity. The song certainly wasn't one of our haphazard Pentecostal songs.

What shocked me most was the congregants all facing the wall, swaying from side to side, and singing in the dark. There were no sudden movements, no hands raised in worship, no moving around in joyful praise. No "Hallelujahs" or "Praise the Lords." I was used to hearing a rousing rendition of "This Little Light of Mine," or maybe one of our made-up songs like "What's the Matter with Jesus, He's Alright." So standing in a devotion service like this one in Newark, New Jersey left me feeling strange. I wondered, was this the kind of worship God requires? Not hearing one word of testimony or one unplanned song in worship was strange to me. Was the way we had been worshipping wrong? This new way of conducting worship service took hold and spread throughout the Pentecostal churches like wildfire.

It has been a long time since I heard someone prophesy in unknown tongues with the interpretation coming forth, edifying the church in a worship service. I remember when people would stand and interpret tongues beginning with, "Thus saith the Lord. . . ." In fact, I cannot remember the last time I heard prophesying during any part of a worship service, of late. Do we do that anymore? Whatever happened to that part of the service? Is it gone forever?

There are gospel artists and church members who still sing the old gospel songs and dress according to the Word of God, 'in moderate apparel.' I thank God for those stalwarts who are not swayed by every new fad. I know times have changed, and people are conducting worship services in jeans and sneakers. I know there are people with tattoos and piercings leading people to Jesus. I know if God can use a donkey, He can use anybody. I know.

Does it matter to God if you shave off the hair on one side of your head and color the remaining hair on the other side of your head purple? With all the horrible events going on in the world today, does God care if you wear earrings all over your body, and tattoo yourself from neck to toe? Are these things important only to us pew-viewers, viewing all these occurrences with shock and awe? Maybe it doesn't matter if people do not want to dress more appropriately for church. Coming from the 'former' church, I believe that after the Holy Ghost is come, there will be a change and a desire to please the Lord.

I can remember the church in its first glory and I saw the changes; the accommodations, resolutions, and tolerations in defiance of, and even downright surrender of church standards. The pressures of this world—not to mention, the empty pews—forced the church to become less stringent and more accommodating to the demands of people. It is as if people said, "I will come and sit in your pews, but only on my terms." The church, fearful of empty pews and closed doors, now accommodates people who have decided they will continue to live in their sins, straddle the fence and, to add insult to injury, bring in more people with that same attitude and mindset. We can only pray that as they sit in their steadfast rebellion, the Word of God will convict, soften their stony hearts and bring deliverance.

Why are we turning the church into a community center? Why do we bring in entertainers, stars and comedians, believing these people will bring in dedicated, consecrated church members? Our Lord and

Savior Jesus Christ said, "My house shall be called a house of prayer." If that's all the church should be, then we do not need to install skating rinks for the children, night clubs for the young adults, or host loud all-night concerts to keep people in the pews. For the smaller churches, the concerts require selling tickets at the door of the church.

When there is a gospel concert at the arena or convention center, we should pay for a ticket and go. We should go because it is a gospel concert. If we want to attend a worship service, then it should be open to the public and free for all to come. Church is where we pray for deliverance, receive Salvation, pray for healing, and hear the Word of God. If we go back to the core basics of the church, we will find our place of worship.

If the church needs to sell dinners and hold thrift clothing sales because the tithes and offerings cannot carry the church's expenses, then leadership should reevaluate their need to exist. Not to boast or to condemn, I will go so far as to say, if the church needs to sell used old clothes, pocketbooks, pots and pans, instead of giving these things away, then something is wrong. The Bible says in Psalms 37:25, *"I have been young, and now am old; yet have I not seen the righteous forsaken, nor his seed begging bread."* A religious leader, whom I highly admire, disagrees with me on closing churches that cannot afford to stay open. She said the church has to stay open by any means necessary. Therefore, if selling dinners, clothes or housewares keep the doors open, she feels nothing is wrong with that. The Bible says in Malachi 3:10, *"Bring ye all the tithes into the storehouse, that there may be meat in mine house, and prove me now herewith, saith the LORD of hosts, if I will not open you the windows of heaven, and pour you out a blessing, that there shall not be room enough to receive it."* If we do as the Lord commands, our churches will not suffer lack and neither will we. Pentecostal church members, we should re-visit this issue.

| CHAPTER 4 |

Come as You Are

Did you know the phrase "Come as you are" is not in the Bible? Many people have used this phrase to protest wearing clothes considered respectable into the House of Prayer. They want the church to allow them to 'come as they are,' and they plan to 'stay as they are' if they decide to become a member of the church. I know one thing; you will not be able to 'stay' in a courthouse or visit a prison dressed provocatively. You will respect their rules if you plan to go there.

In order to wear the most inappropriate apparel to church, people often cherry-pick the Scripture from 1 Samuel 16:7b, *"For man looketh on the outward appearance, but the LORD looketh on the heart."* They take this verse to mean 'I can wear anything I want to wear to church' with the constant refrain, 'God knows my heart.' This is certainly true because what's in the heart comes out. If you do not feel dressed up unless your cleavage is falling out, or your face is made up so much that you look like a clown, then this is what's in your heart.

Back in the day, the church mothers warned young women to not look like Jezebel. How did Jezebel look? The verse 2 Kings 9:30 reads she painted her eyes and tied her head. I do not know what she did to herself, but because it's noted in the Bible, I guess it was more than what the common women were doing. Back in the day, no one ever thought or even dreamed of wearing a pair of jeans to church. Let me just say this, wearing jeans and sneakers to church back in the 1960s would have been thought sacrilegious. Today there are ministers of the Gospel who will not only wear jeans in the pulpit, they will wear ripped up jeans, just to push the envelope. If anyone said anything about it, the minister asks defiantly, "Where in the Bible does it say you can't wear jeans?" Nowhere, sir. The next time you stand before a court judge—some of them believing the Holy Bible an 'ancient book' and not to be adhered to—see if he approves of you standing before him in his courtroom wearing cut up, ripped up jeans. If you were subpoenaed to testify, I guarantee you will be wearing your best Sunday-go-to-meeting church suit with a tie and shiny shoes. If you will respect an earthly authority, why would you disrespect your Heavenly Father by approaching His pulpit in ripped up jeans to deliver the Word? In addition, you as a minister, and carrier of the Word of God, must be an example for our children. If the parents are having a hard time teaching the children how to dress properly for church, seeing you wearing cut up jeans on the pulpit makes their job that much more difficult. Let's discuss if I'm wrong about it; this is just my view from the pew.

Moving into the 2000s, women wearing pants in the Pentecostal church is commonplace. Women wearing makeup slowly became acceptable. The church's rules have become more lax and the standards of apparel in the church are placed a little lower. Progressive Christians cry out, "Don't judge!" Quoting Matthew 7:3, *"And why beholdest thou the mote that is in thy brother's eye, but considerest not the beam that is in thine own eye?"* Using this verse, people say, "Wearing long dresses and cotton stockings does not make anyone more Saved than the praise dancers kicking their legs high over the pews!" The change-makers say, "Show love." In other words, tolerate it; times have changed. Deal with it!

Times really have changed when the young men began attending church wearing their hair in cornrows. Alarmed congregants were in utter shock when the men started wearing earrings and necklaces or gold chains. As time went on, men came to church sporting hairdos styled more beautifully than the women in the church. This was just too much for the old stalwarts to take. We, the pew-viewers, were told to be thankful the brothers are in the church at all. The idea being, "We have to keep the young people encouraged. Let them come as they are."

Incidentally, these were not new brothers coming into the church for the first time. These brothers were always in the church and have been there for years. The brothers came up under the same preaching and teaching we all came under. They just wanted to assimilate more with the outside world and still attend church.

So what was happening? The young people were becoming more defiant and the change in their apparel was the sign that they wanted rules to accommodate their modern styles. The mindset was, "I'm wearing my jeans; I'm wearing my sneakers; I'm wearing my large, loopy earrings with my name written inside them; I'm wearing my tight, short skirts; and whatever else I choose to wear. And if you want me to stay in your church, you have to accept how I wish to dress. After all the Bible says, 'come as you are!'" Because we let the standards slip and tolerated this growing defiance from the younger people in the church, we are in the night, as opposed to 'back in the day.' Because of our lowered standards, church ushers are now holding sheets up and running behind men and women walking down the aisles of the church wearing their pants below their backsides! Do you think we need to discuss this? Let's talk about it.

Not many choirs are wearing robes anymore. Gospel singers, once inspirational and spiritual, sound and look like secular singers; some even more so. Young people don't want to dress old, but they don't have to look like 'pick-ups' either. I know two very well-known Evangelists (women) who once ministered in robes or classy suits. They did not wear any makeup because it was against church rules. Their ministries were so anointed and effective that they changed hearts and minds and brought many lost souls to the Lord. When they became even more popular and their ministries went worldwide, they were told they didn't have to look so 'saved and sanctified.' Not to say they couldn't look nice or wear some makeup for television viewing, but I have observed once they started wearing a little makeup and jewelry, they began to wear *more* makeup and jewelry. One of the evangelists, always a person who preached hard, when she started preaching, makeup ran and smeared all over her face and clothes. Your mind left what she was saying and lingered on the red lipstick and black mascara smeared across her face.

One funny incident, an evangelist preached and sweat ran down her face. She used her handkerchief to wipe the sweat off, but the more she wiped, the more makeup she rubbed off her face. She did not realize that by the end of her sermon, she looked like she used to look when she didn't wear makeup.

I know not all who wear makeup will wear so much that it looks awful; some of us need makeup, I certainly do. Just remember, we should do everything in moderation. We should always try to look nice, respectable and clean. Your appearance matters. In comparison to the old days, the ladies of the church wore no makeup at all. Their dresses were long, and they did not ever show cleavage, shoulders, knees, or toes. At all times, their head had to be covered. I wore lacy doilies on my head for years. I even had doilies in different colors to match the outfits I wore. I may still throw one on my head today, if I feel like it, but I know my daughters would not be caught dead in one.

New times bring new fashions. Today's church members wear risqué outfits that leave even the most liberal members with their mouths hanging open. The young women may wear a nice suit, but the split runs all the way up the thighs. They will tip into the church wearing four-, five-, or even six-inch heels. Why? It is the style. It brings attention to them. They feel like it makes them more attractive. Do you need to be attractive to attend church? I would rather attract Jesus. Yes, Lord, look at me and save my soul from Hell.

No, 'come as you are' is not in the Bible, however Joel 2:32 does tell of the prophet declaring the terrible judgments of the Day of the Lord; God's offer of deliverance is open to 'whosoever shall call upon the name of the Lord.' Isaiah 1:18 offers the invitation to come, though your sins are as scarlet, and He will make them white as snow. Revelation 22:17 gives the invitation into the new Heaven, which says, 'Come! Whosoever will, let him take the water of life freely.' I say, from my view from the pew, no the Bible does not say, 'come as you are' per se, but it does invite you to come and be Saved. Once people gain a closer relationship with the Lord, and have been in the church for a while, they will dress appropriately and honorably, respecting the House of God. This is my prayer.

| CHAPTER 5 |

The Power of the Holy Ghost

"I indeed baptize you with water unto repentance.
But he that cometh after me is mightier than I, whose
shoes I am not worthy to bear: he shall baptize you
with the Holy Ghost, and with fire." **– Matthew 3:11**

The Pentecostal Church *was* the House of Prayer. Not only because of its name 'Pentecost,' but because that was all they used to do back in the early days. As I wrote in my second book, *Screen Door: A Memoir*, the church members would have noon-day prayer, and at times came to our house to pray with my mother in our living room. The prayer warriors stood in a circle, holding hands, and sent up prayers, praises and moans to Heaven.

As someone observing people in the Pentecostal Church, I honestly thought they were making their mouths say words no one could understand. I wanted to know if this was real. I attended tarrying services and prayed to the Lord to be filled with the Holy Ghost. After attending many of these services, I wasn't any closer to being filled. While I am speaking about being filled with the Holy Ghost, I want to say, I do not like the term, 'catch the Spirit.' You do not 'catch' anything! Acts 19:2 reads: *"He said unto them, Have ye received the Holy Ghost since ye believed?"* You 'receive' the Holy Ghost, not 'catch' it.

In Acts 2:3-4, it reads: *"And there appeared unto them cloven tongues like as of fire, and it sat upon each of them. And they were all filled with*

42

the Holy Ghost, and began to speak with other tongues, as the Spirit gave them utterance." It is still happening today! Hallelujah. Amen. A few theologians believe the Holy Ghost evidenced by speaking in other tongues only happened with the Apostles and is no longer happening or needed. When you read the second chapter of Acts, there were more people in the Upper Room besides the Apostles, and all of them were filled.

After receiving Salvation, I then went to everybody I sinned against or didn't like for some reason and apologized to them. I fasted a few days and earnestly prayed believing this is the way to receive the Holy Ghost. One night in November 1979, I attended a prayer meeting at a friend's church. I kneeled down and prayed, and my tongue felt funny and I started speaking in unknown tongues. I stopped praying and looked around, thinking, "I'm doing this on my own." I closed my eyes, and my tongue started stammering and saying words by itself. I was filled! It is real! It really happens! I went home that night feeling light as a feather. I will speak more about the Holy Spirit and Pentecost later in the chapter. In worship services, when the Spirit of the Lord comes, you will feel like you could fly from your seat and praise God forever. When you are filled, you do have a comforter. He is a keeper in times of despair, and the Lord is with you through everything, I mean *everything*!

Living this Saved, Sanctified and Holy Ghost-filled life made people in the community inquire what made me, the Pentecostal person, so different, so peculiar. Telling people of the transformation of my life, and how God has kept me in this dark and evil world, citing Scripture, drew people to seek Salvation. Often the light of the Lord shines in a Saved person's face and prompts people to ask, "You're one of those Saved people, right?" Or when someone uses foul language, a person warns, "Oh, don't curse, that's a church lady right there." People want to know and some are even searching for a better way of life, because the advocate of evil is roaring and seeking whom he may devour. This gives an avenue to witness and talk to people about the way to Salvation.

The 'former' Pentecostal Church held weeknight prayer services, prayer meetings in the homes, prayer tarrying services where people kneeled for hours praying before the Lord. Several times a year there were even shut-in services where members would shut-in the church for days, bringing toothbrushes and maybe pillows, and kneel at the altar fasting and praying. Tarrying services consisted of people praying and waiting on God for the in-filling of the Holy Ghost, which was the next step after receiving Salvation. The prayer warriors, who were older or who we called 'seasoned saints,' prayed with you, standing or sitting next to you, helping to what we call 'pray you through,' sort of like cheering you on or helping you call out to God, until deliverance came. These prayers could last until the wee hours of the morning. Sometimes, people would be so overcome in the prayer that members had to be carried out of the church, and taken home, still praying and speaking in tongues.

Pentecost means fifty, commemorating the time between the day Our Lord and Savior ascended into Heaven after His crucifixion and the day of Pentecost when all that were waiting in the Upper Room were filled with the Holy Spirit. Acts 2:4 reads: *"And they were all filled with the Holy Ghost, and began to speak with other tongues, as the Spirit gave them utterance."* As in the biblical days, the 'former' church people prayed and waited for the Holy Spirit to come and fill them. Acts 2:1 reads: *"And when the day of Pentecost was fully come, they were all with one accord in one place."*

Only after the in-filling takes place can you receive power to witness, preach, prophesy, and do the work that the Lord has anointed you to do. Acts 1:8 reads: *"But ye shall receive power, after that the Holy Ghost is come upon you: and ye shall be witnesses unto me both in Jerusalem, and in all Judaea, and in Samaria, and unto the uttermost part of the earth."*

Receiving the power of the Holy Ghost is what set the Pentecostal Church apart from other churches. To be present when the Holy Spirit is poured out in any service is the most miraculous and powerful atmosphere ever. You lose control of your emotions and just want to cry like a baby, because the Love of God is so strong, so profound; you feel such joy, such unspeakable joy. As you dwell in the Spirit of God, you just want to stay in His presence and never leave. After the in-filling of the Holy Spirit, every part of the Pentecostal's life has changed. The born again Christian is now in the world but not of the world.

In the 'former' church, there was the laying on of hands. People would stand before the servant of God for prayer. The servant anoints the person's head with oil and lays his hand on the person. Sometimes the power of the Holy Spirit causes the person to fall on the floor. While on the floor, the person is laying there under the power of God. We called this being 'slain in the Spirit.' Let me tell you from experience, being slain is nothing to be afraid of. While slain in the Spirit, you can hear everything around you, but you cannot get up. Some people are still praising the Lord while slain, some just lay quiet. Oh, the joy and peace you feel while lying in the presence of God. Quite a deliverance in many areas of people's lives has occurred while slain in the Lord. Many have received the in-filling of the Holy Ghost while slain in the Spirit.

When speaking of the Holy Spirit, many people who are confused by it and want to know more about it, also want to know how to receive it. In many churches, the receiving of the Holy Spirit is never taught. These churches are like the people Apostle Paul encountered in Acts 19:2. *"He said unto them, Have ye received the Holy Ghost since ye believed? And they said unto him, We have not so much as heard whether there be any Holy Ghost."*

I'm just a pew-viewer, so I can only express what I myself have experienced. After I received the Holy Ghost, speaking in other tongues as the Spirit gave utterance, I found I had a stronger desire to live and work for the Lord. The Holy Spirit is also known as the Comforter, and I can truly say He comforts, He consoles, He bring things back to your remembrance. For me, when I'm down or discouraged, a song will come to mind or a verse of the Scripture; sometimes, even a message that was preached some time before will come to mind and encourage me. When there is a death in the family, maybe someone very close, the feeling of grief and despair overtakes you. You sit, cry but when you are filled with the Holy Spirit, a feeling of comfort comes over you and helps you endure the pain. In order to deal with their grief, I notice family members who are not Saved grab a cigarette, a drink, pills or even drugs in times of bereavement.

I wrote in my book, *Screen Door: A Memoir*, of the death of a sister who was one year younger than me. She was struck by lightning at the age of thirteen. Then I had another sister born eight months after this sister's death. She died at the age of thirty-five in her sleep. Losing two sisters, both younger than me, made my grief almost insurmountable. I thought I would never laugh again. My youngest sister was such a sweet person, and she left behind four little children who loved her beyond words. After the funeral and burial, I sat in my living room thinking of the first time I saw my baby sister in her crib sleeping so soundly, and then thirty-five years later, seeing her lying in her coffin, sleeping so soundly. I wondered why both my sisters were taken from us so unexpectedly. I could easily have been angry with God, or justified in my grief, but instead I sat in my living room, crying. The Lord wrapped my heart and mind in His Love and comforted me with peace that surpassed all understanding (Philippians 4:7).

When trouble comes, such as court dates, homelessness, tight financial restraints, bodily harm, divorce, illnesses, death in the family, and in my case, sudden terrorist attacks, the Comforter will remind you that there is a mighty God and He will bring you out of all your troubles. In 2 Corinthians 4:7-9, *"But we have this treasure in earthen vessels, that the excellency of the power may be of God, and not of us. We are troubled on every side, yet not distressed; we are perplexed, but not in despair; Persecuted, but not forsaken; cast down, but not destroyed."* Yes, I've fallen short; yes, I've sinned; yes, I suffer ailments and sickness; but I am not left in despair, I am not without hope. This is why I am so happy to have been brought up in the 'former' Pentecostal Church. If it had not been for the tarrying services, the all-night prayer services, the Spirit-filled worship services, and the anointed sermons, I cannot imagine where I would be today. Can we discuss bringing back tarrying services? Should we continue to seek for the in-filling of the Holy Ghost today? Do you think the Holy Ghost is still needed in this day and time?

People *worked* with the converts back then. They prayed with them, tarried with them, followed-up with them, and taught them the way of the cross as well as the ways of the church. New converts were obedient back then. They came humble and had a willingness to do all that is required of them to receive Salvation and to live a Sanctified and holy life.

The Pentecostal faith stands and rests on the in-filling of the Holy Ghost. Our anthem is 'We are Saved, Sanctified and Filled with the Precious Holy Ghost.' The Holy Ghost gives us power to live holy. St. John 14:26 reads: *"But the Comforter, which is the Holy Ghost, whom the Father will send in my name, he shall teach you all things, and bring all things to your remembrance, whatsoever I have said unto you."*

Our faith is belief that Our Lord and Savior Jesus Christ is the Son of God, who died on the cross for the cleansing of our sins. To be Saved is to be born again of the Spirit of God, and once born again, faithfully live a Sanctified and holy life. To be Sanctified is to be set apart and set aside from sinful living and to be a witness to the world. To be filled with the Holy Ghost is to receive the power of the Holy Spirit from Heaven.

A Sanctified person is delivered from vices that defile the body such as drinking alcohol, smoking and taking drugs. A Saved person is also delivered from using foul language, lying, and a whole host of evil-doings and dealings against our fellow man. A Sanctified, Holy Ghost-filled person has received power to abstain from sins. To be Sanctified and Holy Ghost filled gives you power to live right (St. John 17:14). A holy and Sanctified life must be lived inwardly, which will show outwardly.

I admit there are some traditions in the Pentecostal faith I feel should never change, such as the church doctrine itself. First and foremost, the church should be a place of prayer. Our sermons, prayers, songs, and testimonies should stem from Scripture. We should follow the Bible, which today's lawmakers now call an antiquated book. I believe the Bible should be the foundation for any worship service. Although I prefer our worship songs to derive from the Holy Bible, I do not consider myself to be an old traditionalist. Yes, I like some of the new worship songs, too.

Some rituals, I believe, will have to change due to the passage of time and the onset of technology. We should not stray from the teachings of the Bible just to stay current. We can still revere God in holiness with our praise and worship without moving away from the

Scriptures. With the Holy Spirit leading our hearts and minds, our worship should be even more spiritual and uplifting.

At times, the Holy Spirit might take over a service so strongly the minister does not have a chance to preach the Sunday morning sermon. Someone's testimony or song reached the people at the point of their need and the church just goes up in praise. To be in a service when this takes place has got to be the next best thing to being in Heaven! Whew! Talking about a time; talking about a good time! I cannot describe the liberation, the freedom, the joy when the Holy Spirit takes over a service. Praise Him!

| CHAPTER 6 |

Clothed in Your Right Mind

A pastor once proclaimed, "It seem like they emptied out the insane asylum and they all came to my church!" In this day and age, we see so many people with mental illnesses. So many people are mentally ill or even insane and do not even know it. Some people have and have not been diagnosed with schizophrenia, bi-polar disorder, mild retardation, or depression. People with some of these illnesses are able to function in society without much attention drawn to them. Only when they act out in a peculiar way does society take notice; otherwise, their illness lays dormant.

In prior years, the black community did not seek help from psychiatrists, psychologists or mental institutions because it brought a stigma to the person. Another reason was financial inability to seek the much needed medical attention. Therefore, the church received many individuals with these mental illnesses and disabilities. Untold millions of alcoholics, along with depressed and suicidal people, were prayed for and these spirits were cast out by the laying on of hands by ministers and prayer warriors in the church. However, in some of the 'latter' churches, people are not taught about praying for the insane or people oppressed by the enemy.

Receiving the in-filling of the Holy Ghost gives you power to do the Lord's work. Even the ushers need to be filled with the Holy Spirit because they are in contact with different kinds of people entering the church. A friend of mine told me of a time in her church when her pastor was praying for a woman that needed deliverance. As he prayed for her, she fell out and started shaking and screaming. In the 'former' church, ushers were just as powerful as the pastor. They would surround the woman, holding sheets to wrap the woman in, because at times people being saved are flailing and kicking. By pleading the blood and praying with the pastor or minister, the person will receive deliverance.

The pastor of my friend's church waved for the ushers to come and assist him, but instead, the ushers ran out of the church, as well as half the church. Someone called 911 and the paramedics came and tried to do vitals on the woman who was screaming and shaking on the floor. This situation would not have happened if the church was taught through the Word of God, and were filled with the Holy Ghost, on how to handle someone in this state.

In the biblical days, situations with the insane and mentally ill occurred. We read in Matthew 17 where an insane boy was brought for prayer and the Disciples could not help him. Our Lord and Savior seemed exasperated that the Disciples or anyone under his teachings could not help the boy. We read in verses 17-21: *"Then Jesus answered and said, O faithless and perverse generation, how long shall I be with you? How long shall I suffer you? Bring him hither to me. And Jesus rebuked the devil; and he departed out of him: and the child was cured from that very hour. Then came the disciples to Jesus apart, and said, Why could not we cast him out? And Jesus said unto them, Because of your unbelief: for verily I say unto you, If ye have faith as a grain of mustard seed, ye shall say unto this mountain, Remove hence to yonder place; and it shall remove; and nothing shall be impossible unto you. Howbeit this kind goeth not out but by prayer and fasting."*

There are many instances in the Bible where the insane and the troubled came to the Lord and they were delivered. As ministers and even lay persons, we cannot have the spirit of fear and doubt in our hearts when dealing with troubled people. You need the power of the Holy Ghost and faith to handle these situations. This is why church is no joke, it is serious business. People run to the church for help and we as members should be prayed up, fasted up and ready to receive them. The mentally disturbed seem to be more prevalent today than at any other time. People are trying to deal with their mental torment by using drugs, alcohol, sexual activities, and perversion. When terrible violence occurs by an oppressed person, most of the time the cause is the person went off his medication.

Among everybody sharing the pew you are sitting in, some may not be clothed in their right mind. Anything can tick them off and they can become violent or perform unseemly acts. At my view from the pew, I have seen people who had to be restrained. The members of the church often times had to encircle the disturbed person, plead the blood and cast out devils from that tormented person who beforehand was sitting in the pew like everybody else. You need power with God to deal with this very real enemy. Ephesians 6:12 reads: *"For we wrestle not against flesh and blood, but against principalities, against powers, against the rulers of the darkness of this world, against spiritual wickedness in high places."* It's sad to say, just like the church that ran out and dialed 911 out of fear, many young people have never experienced demons being cast out of people.

| CHAPTER 7 |

Preach, Preacher!

As I mentioned earlier, preachers were firebrand, hollering, singing, dynamic ministers who brought forth the Word of God with such torchy oratory, their voices would literally lift you out of your seat. They would rear back, hold one ear and let it out, humming, yelling and stammering words of inspiration, instruction and encouragement. The minister's billowing full robes flowed and swayed as he or she glided across the pulpit delivering the message. Oh, the passion, sweating, breathing, and grunting the preacher exerted back in those days, with the pouring of the anointing all over him or her, compelling the hearts of men to obey.

The Pentecostal Church ministers, at times, may receive a revelation from God in the middle of a sermon. Yes, the preacher may start out with his notes, but in the midst of his sermon, a revelation may come to him and the anointing will fill him up so much that he is able to give the church a bit of wisdom that was not thought of before. When the minister is in the Spirit and preaches under the anointing, the Word comes to life; people are delivered, healed and filled with the Holy Spirit. Any church, not just Pentecostals, may receive the anointing like that if the praise and worship is filled with the Holy Spirit.

Pastors and ministers who pray, separate themselves, and meditate on the Word of God before delivering their messages, seeking the mind of God, want the congregation to receive from the Lord. I see a marked difference from the 'former' days of old in this regard. I have seen ministers go before the Lord before they impart their sermons, fasting and praying. Unfortunately, I do not sense that this sacrifice and submission may occur with all preachers. It appears to me that some of the preachers' messages have been re-mixed, rehearsed and, at times, re-hashed.

Sure sermons can be told over again, for instruction and edification; this may happen on occasion. There are even times when an old sermon is preached again, in a new way, with new revelations and insights revealed; that happens occasionally, too. However, there are times when a minister finds a verse, invents a clever catchy theme and runs with a message.

The 'latter' day ministers may speak for one to two hours (or longer) on a topic that they know will get people's emotions riled up. Topics like: broken relationships, divorce, politics, finance, or building your own business are lectured to show people how to live a better life. I don't know about you, but it has been a long time since I heard a message about fire and brimstone, Hell and the rapture.

What is really sad is to see ministers making the altar call at the very end of one of their sermons, as if it was an afterthought. This should be the whole reason for preaching in the first place! Sometimes the minister jerks back to the podium, as if he just remembered, and says: *"Is there anyone here who desires to accept the Lord as your personal savior?"*

In the 'former' church, when the great Reverend Billy Graham, or even the late Bishop Elnora Smith, in the smaller Pentecostal church in Harlem, preached the way of Salvation for over an hour, it was not jarring when the invitation to the cross was called; it was a smooth transition. To be fair, there are ministers and pastors on television today preaching the way to Salvation, and you can feel the anointing and the urgency of the message before they go right into the sinner's prayer and receiving people into the body of Christ. This, I feel, should be done all the time.

The preachers of the Pentecostal faith were men and women who imparted the Word of God with fervor and depth. They interpreted the Holy Bible under the anointing and spoke from experience. When they finished preaching, sometimes they were drenched in sweat as they returned to their seats. Back in the 'former' church, there were ushers who would at times pass them a tissue or a glass of water. After preaching so hard, the ministers opened the altar for prayer, and they laid hands on each and every person on line! They worked hard and did not rush the service, making sure everything he or she thought was required was done.

I didn't see adjutants, or I should say I didn't notice any, carrying the preacher's bags, coats and Bibles up to the pulpit. There were no special assistants to the preacher actually taking a seat on the pulpit for the sole purpose of wiping the preacher's forehead, opening his Bible for him, or his laptop, and passing dry handkerchiefs to the preacher every fifteen minutes. I never saw, until recently, an adjutant carrying a hot pot of tea on a silver tray up to the pulpit, pouring a cup for the preacher after he preached! I think that's a bit much, but that is just my view from the pew. A poor pew, I might add, in a small Pentecostal church in the hood. You can have your spot of tea in the office after service. What do you think?

Another disturbing occurrence is the security detail some of the preachers require in the larger churches. The armed security detail escorts the pastor everywhere because his life might be in danger, in the church! Some of these pastors flash very expensive jewelry, wear very expensive clothes and shoes, and ride in very expensive cars. Some of them live in mansions and own jets, but their churches are still in the hood.

While they are ministering, instead of the congregation receiving the Word of deliverance, they are looking at the preacher's gold, diamond-crusted watch, pinky rings, snakeskin shoes, diamond studs in his ears, or his custom made suit. The security detail sits in the aisles and front seats of the sanctuary looking over the congregation for possible threats. My view from the pew is I wonder if the Lord is pleased with his messengers, pastors and ministers walking down the aisle of the sanctuary with a squadron of armed guards.

The Word of God does read in 3rd John 1:2, *"Beloved, I wish above all things that thou mayest prosper and be in health, even as thy soul prospereth."* I wonder if we can remain humble and not become full of pride by wearing a whole bunch of gaudy jewelry and fancy clothes. Having armed security around the pastor makes it very hard to shake his hand or to come close to him. Some of the pastors came from nothing, and never had expensive clothes. After becoming successful in their ministerial careers, they may overdo it and become indignant if anyone mentions the preacher might be too materialistic. In fact, some preachers are very defensive and cite how nobody says anything when a rock star rides in a limousine, or a superstar has his own Lear jet. But some of these preachers fail to see that preaching the Word is to preach to the poor. St. Luke 4:18 reads: *"The Spirit of the Lord is upon me, because he hath anointed me to preach the gospel to the poor; he hath sent me to heal the brokenhearted, to preach deliverance to the captives, and recovering of sight to the blind, to set at liberty them that are bruised."* Your entire purpose for ministering is to benefit the poor and needy. Not that you need to be poor with the poor, but you should at least be humble and reachable because God hates even a proud look (Proverbs 6:17)!

| CHAPTER 8 |

If Anyone Desires the Office of Pastor

I am fortunate to have known a few really dedicated pastors in my lifetime. They would give the shirt off their backs for their members. I have seen pastors walk out in a snow storm and bring groceries to families in need. What motivates them to do this? They say, "God sent me." Pastors care for the sheep and have a heart for the souls who attend the church. The pastor's job requires dedication, service, patience, and love for the congregation.

In the Pentecostal Church, the position of pastor does not necessarily require education or seminary. It would be wonderful if they did have *some* education, but it is not required. If the person declares he is 'called' to preach, or 'called' to be a pastor, he usually can be ordained to start up a church. Now, as an old-time Pentecostal pew-viewer, I sat under quite a few pastors who did not finish high school. But I must say, if they are anointed, filled with the Spirit, and the Lord uses them to minister effectively, it usually works out. I certainly have seen people without education lead a successful church. Most importantly, they have led many souls to Christ, and some of those converts they have led were educated and have started their own ministries.

Believe it or not, education is not the problem most of the time. What often causes church conflicts are leaders who are enthralled in bad financial dealings, in-fighting, jealousies, grievous sins, and desires to be rich and famous. I am no authority on this, I am just speaking from what I've seen as a pew-viewer. I believe if these leaders were 'born again' their very nature would have changed, and these kinds of problems would not exist. I believe a 'born again' Christian will not cheat the church financially, for example. Of course, people may argue that they know of a 'born again' pastor who cheated on his wife, lied on finance papers, used drugs, etc. I say, I wonder if that person was really 'born again.' If the pastor was 'born again,' he would have a new nature; old things would have passed away.

The reason many people become pastors in the first place is because they did not agree with the way their prior church was administered by the pastor. The disgruntled church member may have seen how pastoring was done, and thought it couldn't be that hard, so he opens his own church. When opening their own church, many in the Pentecostal Church will take half of the membership of the old church with him, who agreed with his disgruntled issues and followed him.

Many women opened their own church because their original church did not believe in women preachers, or their original church did not believe in divorce and remarriage. Other reasons for opening individual churches may have been caused by disagreements with the clothing restrictions or other church protocols. It is said, one cannot be a good leader if you cannot be a good follower. So as you may surmise, some of these bad followers became bad leaders.

Some of these churches led by disgruntled former members have become non-effective churches, led by people who have very few followers. How do I know this? I have seen these churches in every city and state I have visited. I believe some of these people were not called by God to be pastors; this is apparent by their attitudes toward the people they encounter. When the bad leaders were followers, they did not respect leadership and were contrary in many ways. Now that they are leaders themselves, or made themselves leaders, they are mean, disagreeable, dominating, and full of pride. Needless to say, they do not follow peace with all men as the Bible instructs in Hebrews 12:14, *"Follow peace with all men, and holiness, without which no man shall see the Lord."*

I found quite a few people desiring the position of pastor because they have no other skill or education to do anything else. Where else can you acquire the prestige and respect of being called Pastor or Reverend, without training or education? Just because we are Pentecostals, does not mean we have to be ignorant and uneducated to preach the Gospel. Yes, God can use the uneducated, after all, the Disciples were uneducated; however, Apostle Paul was an educated man, and he was able to express himself much more effectively and go into places and speak to people who he would otherwise not have access to. On the other hand, if we possess many degrees in academia, we have to be mindful to remain humble and let the Lord speak through us. Acquiring degrees sometimes leads one to lean on his own intellect instead of following the leading of the Lord.

Back in the 'former' church, preachers who opened their own churches, without an organized overhead, or proper training and education, were called jackleg preachers. In the 'latter' church, these kinds of preachers are called 'Lone Rangers.' Some 'Lone Rangers' may have a 'Tonto' following along with him. In the Pentecostal faith, the 'Lone Ranger' usually heads an independent church without a governing body. Most of them do not have members or even a church building. Some 'Lone Rangers' have quit their regular jobs. From my view from the pew, I have seen some of them quit their jobs because they did not like their jobs to begin with. Some were doing manual labor or held down mundane jobs that did not pay much. Consequently, heading a church, no matter how small, was their way out. I have found most 'Lone Rangers' to be frustrated, always conjuring up schemes to make a quick buck, and unable to pay their bills. They are usually unemployed and depend on gifts and offerings to get by. So they seek speaking engagements in other churches to make a living. I am not going to say saving souls is not their priority; I'll leave that up to them and God. Also, I'm not saying all independent 'Lone Rangers' are crooked. There are those who sincerely desire to be ministers and diligently work to please the Lord. However, they need to, but refuse to, sit under seasoned clergy and receive the training and development needed to become a successful minister. So the 'Lone Ranger and Tonto' go forth, damaging, being a burden, bringing hurt and instability into the churches.

Pastoring a small storefront church that is not large or affluent enough to support a pastor and his family is problematic. The larger churches which have salaried, full-time pastors, you would think would be more available to their congregants to do the Lord's work. To the contrary, many of them rarely go out into the communities, unless they have speaking engagements. They sparingly spend time with the young people of their congregation, and seldom conduct any ministry outside the church unless it is to sell their books or travel to conferences or pastor symposiums. In addition, if you as a member call some of these full-time, salaried pastors, they may have their telephones set to voice mail, and he might get back to you or have somebody get back to you at a later time. Most of these 'full-time' pastors are not out in the community, touching the people, like Jesus did.

Full-time pastoring should free up the pastor's time to visit his members who are in the hospitals, nursing homes or the prisons. The pastor should be able to show up at the court houses, visit the shut-ins and even visit other churches. If the church is large enough, the pastor may send the missionary team out to do all these tasks. This is my view: some ministers were never sent but went. Remember, again I said, "I think" some ministers do not have or cannot attain any other vocation, so they go into ministry. They choose to be preachers or pastors because this is the only way they can earn a living. This profession gives them stature and prestige, and it's not that hard to get a license to minister.

I really do believe when Our Lord and Savior Jesus Christ calls someone to pastor, he selects someone with a vocation, because it shows the person is willing to work and earn a living. Do you know of anyone in the Bible Jesus called to follow Him that wasn't working? I do not recall anyone the Lord ever called to discipleship that wasn't already occupied.

We know that even Jesus Himself was a carpenter and so was His earthly father. The Disciples may not have been well educated like Apostle Paul, but they were called because they were willing to work and willing to follow Him. I do not believe the Disciples followed Jesus because they were looking for a livelihood and prestige. When the

Disciples gave up their occupations and followed Jesus, they believed Jesus called them to save the world.

This may sound funny, but there are a whole lot of ministers out there preaching who received their license off the Internet. Some of these preachers haven't sat under anybody for more than a year. Some were, and still are, church-hoppers—who are like chiefs with no Indians. They go from church to church trying to get a night to preach for an offering. It's so sad. They may call themselves apostles, prophets or prophetesses, and some even call themselves bishops. The office of bishop is the overseer of several churches. These bishops do not even have one church, but they use the title of bishop to appear more prestigious.

The Bible instructs in 1 Timothy 3:1-7, if one desires the office of a bishop, desires a good thing. The person cannot be a novice and must have a good reputation inside and outside of the church. Today, the office of bishop has been so desecrated that it grieves your heart. There are many young people, who have not pastored a church for very long, calling themselves bishop. Why are we allowing the standard of the title of bishop to be lowered? Should we restore the requirements as instructed in the Bible? Let's talk about it.

| CHAPTER 9 |

If Anyone Desires the Office of Co-Pastor

Around the 1980s and 1990s, a new titled position presented itself in the Pentecostal Church: Co-pastor. We already had assistant pastors, which are not in the Bible either. However, most assistant pastors were not a relative of the pastor and usually took over the reins of the church if and when the pastor became incapacitated. Co-pastors, on the other hand, tend to always be the wife of a pastor. Co-pastorship came into play when many male pastors wanted their wives to work beside them in the ministry.

This is not funny, but I remember so clearly a television pastor who put his wife up before the cameras to start her co-pastorship. She looked like a deer in front of headlights. Some wives tried to be as dynamic and didactic as their husbands, when actually they were normally shy and introverted. Many of these wives were never called to pastor and had to grow into the position. Unfortunately, more often than not, the wife does not have the heart of a pastor. In fact, they are competing for their husband's time and attention with the church.

I'm not judging, just saying what I see. I said earlier, in an 'organized' church, people vying for the positions of pastor and assistant pastor were selected by the board of the church. The board makes these selections to make sure there is continuance of the church functions if something should happen to the pastor. In most small Pentecostal churches there are no boards. The pastor rules and decides who will be the assistant pastor. In the case of co-pastors, this rule falls through the cracks because what usually happens, when the pastor dies or cannot continue, the church splits up because all of the members do not necessarily want to be pastored by the wife. Rarely does a church carry on under the co-pastor wife. I know of one instance when the male pastor died and his wife took over the church. The church is now a whole different place than when the pastor was alive. Most of the members left, and the rules and standards of the church have woefully fallen.

On the other hand, I know of a woman who pastored a church in Harlem for years, however, her husband was not in the ministry. He didn't stand in the way of her assistant pastor taking over the reins of the church, who happened to be a man. We need to re-visit the co-pastorship issue and see if this benefits the church.

There are many women pastors in the Pentecostal faith. Women holding positions of leadership in the church fought an uphill battle, and believe it or not are still fighting. Women preaching, teaching and leading congregations in the 'former' church were subjected to being relegated to speaking from the floor of the sanctuary instead of standing behind the podium; that is, if she was allowed to speak at all.

More and more women began leading congregations, even though the Pentecostal Church as a whole still did not give them their full respect and honor. The women ministers were not respected in their rightful titles as Reverend or Pastor, but rather referred to as missionary or sister. The men clergy seemed intimidated by women who wished to lead. These intimidated men considered these women 'loose women,' as I mentioned earlier when I spoke about Bishop T.D. Jakes's message, "Woman Thou Art Loosed." It was widely believed that women were not called to preach. But as more and more women began preaching and pastoring churches, the men clergy slowly began to accept the inevitable.

At the base of it all was the belief that women could not handle the work of running a church because of their propensity to get pregnant. After all, she couldn't possibly baptize people during her 'time of the month,' which would make her unclean. Women are to be mothers, a help to her husband, and work behind the scenes like the women in the Bible did with the Disciples. Paul, the great apostle, wrote in his epistles that women are to be quiet in the church. And if she has a question, she should ask her husband at home. I know for certain if the women of the black Pentecostal church are quiet, all you would hear are old men and babies.

A man whose pastor is a woman has to be secure in his manhood. His machismo cannot be offended by a woman in leadership. He is not called to the ministry; she is, so he submits himself under her leadership. In the Bible, a warrior named Barak would not move or fight unless the Prophetess Deborah, a married woman, went with him. He wasn't concerned about how it looked to others, he was concerned that she had a God-given ministry and he knew he would be well served to follow her (Judges chapters 4 & 5). I find in the 'latter' church, many men will not sit under a woman pastor. You will find more men in a church if the pastor is a man. I don't care how much you may call the pastor's wife 'co-pastor'; if the pastor dies and the wife takes over, most of the men in the church will take off.

Most of the smaller, storefront Pentecostal churches are headed up by women. Often the women started the church because elsewhere her leadership would not be acknowledged. Many times, the women pastors' husbands are either not in the church or hold no position of leadership in the church. He is not necessarily a wimp, as some may think. Most of these men are secure enough in their manhood to believe their wives are called to the ministry by God, and they have decided to submit themselves under their wives' leadership. To be honest, I know of no man whose wife is the pastor and he is called co-pastor. While there are many male assistant pastors, remember, most of them are not related to the pastor.

What I find disconcerting, from my view on the pew, is knowing of a talented, intelligent, anointed, and consecrated woman of God, willing to do the work of the Lord, who has to sit in the pew instead of leading the church because her church does not believe in women preachers. While her husband, on the other hand, an overbearing boar, who is not a people person, with non-existent communication skills, and who does not possess a deep love and concern for the people of his congregation, is the pastor. In fact, if he had his druthers, he would rather roll his boat out to the lake and go fishing. The congregants see that the wife is a prayer warrior and a consecrated woman of God, and thus feel cheated. Instead of having an outstanding pastor, they have to settle for a mediocre one because of gender. The Bible says in Jeremiah 3:15, *"And I will give you pastors according to mine heart, which shall feed you with knowledge and understanding."* That is all we need in the 'latter' church, a pastor who will feed us, no matter the gender.

| C H A P T E R   1 0 |

iPad Packing Preachers

In the Disciples' day, they preached and taught the Word of God differently than, let's say, in Moses's and Isaiah's day. Of course, the Word had not changed, it's the way it was delivered that changed. Moses used stone tablets. In Jesus's day, the Scriptures were on scrolls. We, the 'former' church, had the Bible in book form. The 'latter' churches now have iPads, laptops and other digital, technological gadgets with Bible apps in them. Fewer ministers now say, "Take out your Bibles and turn with me to. . . ."

Even the ministers walk up to the pulpits with laptops and iPads to deliver the message. The need to memorize where the books of the Bible are located went the way of memorizing telephone numbers. Just type in the book, chapter and verse, and you are there! I realize you have to move with the times; what I have a problem with, as an old pew-viewer, is the message preached and the motivation behind it. If you are being 'carried away with every wind or doctrine,' my question is, do we have to be carried away with you? Can we just receive the straight message from the Bible without all the modern day flair and showmanship? For example, do we really need a live lion on stage to emphasize a sermon? Do we have to roll a king size bed onto the pulpit to be taught a message on marriage? Does the preacher have to be popular, famous and flamboyant in order to get the message across? Do we have to lower the standards of the church to be relevant in this day and age? I keep asking that last question because I am still searching for an answer.

Even though we are technologically advanced, the same sins still exist. Are the sins less sinful because we are more educationally advanced?

Are we so technologically proficient and educationally advanced that we forget who is in charge and who we are here to serve? We will never be smarter than God. He created us and knows more about us than we know about ourselves. In 2 Kings 5:10, Elisha told the servants of a man to go and tell their master, who was grievously suffering from a very bad skin condition, to dip himself seven times in the dirty Jordan and be healed. The man became angry because he didn't want to dip one big toe into the dirty Jordan one time, not to mention seven times! The man complained suggesting other cleaner, closer bodies of water the prophet might consider him to use.

The sick man felt further dishonored by the prophet because the prophet did not come personally and pronounce healing over his wretched body. After all, he was an important man, who should be respected and honored. As he kept complaining, his servants responded, (I'm improvising) "My goodness, if he asked you to do a hard thing, wouldn't you do it? All he asks you to do is dip in the Jordan seven times and you would be healed!" The man humbled himself and dipped his body in the dirty Jordan seven times, and his skin became as a baby's skin!

Some of the 'latter' church ministers walk in pride with their iPads and degrees. Like I said in an earlier chapter, some preachers have adjutants, valets and security detail whose sole purpose is to assist the preacher. If the Lord asked the iPad packing preacher, who is well educated in seminary and highly regarded by church officials, to take off his Evan Picone jacket, gold watch and expensive jewelry, and commanded him to go down to the dirty shelter and sit with an old discouraged man, would the preacher do it without complaining? Would the preacher suggest cleaner places to meet sinners to do the same work? Would the preacher carry the Bible in book form, because the old man down at the shelter may not have an iPad to follow along, to show the old man the way to Salvation? Would the preacher do it?

| CHAPTER 11 |

Family Churches

My starting point in the church may not be your starting point. I can't say my 'former church' and the way church was conducted back then is your 'former church.' Your 'former church' might have started in later years. You might have arrived in the church and received Salvation right when they were singing, "Stomp!", a song released by Kirk Franklin and God's Property. Your 'former' church may have been when devotional songs were displayed on the church walls through projectors. Men wearing (braided) cornrows in their hair and earrings in their ears to worship services may not have been a total shock to you. I ask then, compared to your 'former' church, how do you see the church now? Is it not in your eyes in comparison of it as nothing?

I do believe the 'former' church, when I was growing up, seemed more genuine and sincere. It just seemed to me that people came into the church, received Salvation and their lives were actually changed. Maybe I was too young and naive to recognize hypocrites. People just seemed to *want* to be different from the world back then, not more *like* the world. It was apparent to me that people came into the church, turned their lives over to Our Lord and Savior Jesus Christ, and actually stopped drinking alcohol, stopped smoking and lived a righteous life.

Everything about the Pentecostal members, even their very appearance, was different. People had such dedication and attended church more than once a week back then. The outreach ministry was fierce; people had a zest and a zeal for the work of God. I can remember when church members would visit homes for prayer. There were all-night prayer meetings in the church and noon-day prayers in the homes. I remember when church members came into my home and conducted noon-day prayers.

At the time my mother received Salvation in her life, I was four or five years old. The first thing I noticed as a young child was the superficial changes. My mother stopped smoking and drinking. These may be small things, but this was something I noticed immediately, as a small child. Then the weekend parties stopped, no more dancing and rock-n-roll records played in our home.

The intrinsic changes were significant! We recognized there is a God, a power greater than us. We believe God created the whole world and all that is therein. We also believe there is a Heaven and a Hell. Living daily, we prayed we did not commit any sin that would send us to Hell. The bishops and pastors preached the ways we should and could please God so as not to become a sinner and be bound for Hell. We tried our best to live the Scripture which says, "We are in the world, but not of the world." Specifically, John 17:14 reads: *"I have given them thy word; and the world hath hated them, because they are not of the world, even as I am not of the world."*

Now that we have reviewed the extrinsic and intrinsic differences of the Pentecostal faith, we can now continue to discuss how I see the faith has evolved into what it is today. People who fought and lost the fight against the stringent rules of the Pentecostal faith began to leave the church and opened their own churches. This brought forth the proliferation of 'family' churches. There are so many family churches you would think every family has their own personal church.

The proliferation of family churches probably started from the Pentecostals due to its non-denominational aspects and the lack of overhead or organized church overseers. If you are not taking part in the ritualistic rules under a denomination, in addition to being a 'Lone Ranger,' the beliefs and non-conforming attributes may lead to creating a family church. A family church is a church filled with people who are related to each other. Usually, the pastor is the father or mother, and the children are the church members, maybe grandparents and grandchildren, aunts and uncles, too. In some of these 'family' churches, almost all the members are relatives or extended relatives of the pastor. In most organized churches, there are about five to ten separate families in the church, holding various positions in the church. In the family church, you may not see more than one family in one Pentecostal church.

Running a family church is difficult in so many ways because, just like running a family in a home, you know each relative intimately. Someone joining some of these family churches, and not related to anyone in the church, will certainly find it hard being a contributing member. No matter how long you have known the pastor or other members of the church, if you are not related to the family, your contribution becomes suspect at best. You will always be considered optional. The non-relative member may find out that any input given in the church will not be received as readily as a relative's input.

As a non-related member, you only have the pastor's ear when you see him. On the other hand, the family has his ear at the church and at home. Favoritism and nepotism run rampant in most family churches; thus, leaving a once dedicated, non-related member feeling uninspired to contribute because of the cliquish atmosphere in the church. A member who is not related to the pastor who may feel like a true contributing member of the church, take heed: Do not dare disagree with anyone in the family. Do not try and discuss your disagreement with a family member about another family member in the church. You will surely find out that 'blood is thicker than water.'

Another discouraging facet of sitting under a pastor in a family church is that steadfast rules and standards might change to accommodate a member of the pastor's family. What was wrong and sinful before may suddenly be alright, or not considered a sin, because a member of the ruling family was found doing it.

Speaking from my view from the pew, there are older lay members in the black Pentecostal church who consider the church 'their' church, whether it is a family church or not. What do I mean by that? Older, long-standing members will refer to the church as 'my church,' as in "I would like to invite you to my church." Or, "I've been a member of my church for over thirty years." Older congregants believe because they have been in the church for so long, and contributed tithes and offerings for years, this affords them vested interest in the church and thus makes them an invaluable member of the church. Younger members can take it or leave it and might resort to church-hopping, but that's another story. Older people will stay in a church until death do they part, if they feel wanted, appreciated and loved. They know they will not be around too much longer, and want to believe their church, the place they love so much, and where they have invested so much into, is their home away from home. The church is sometimes called their church-home. They believe their pastor will preach their funeral and remember them as an honored and dedicated member of the church.

It is so sad to see the faces of these poor older members when reality sets in and they realize they were not considered honored and dedicated church members, but rather they were considered 'guests' of the family church. The older member may have taught Sunday school for twenty years, or headed up the pastor's aide auxiliary for several years; but it does not matter, because if one of the family members of the church wishes to have them removed from an auxiliary for some arbitrary reason, they are out. To add salt to the wound, older unrelated members of some 'family' churches or even some regular churches might find out, to their chagrin, that they have no say or power in the church at all.

Because the seniors may not be able to give big tithes or may need financial assistance every now and then, often the older members are just tolerated, because most 'latter' churches would rather have younger people to help move the church forward. Older people are often considered a drain on the church. In addition, seniors tend to hold on to traditions that the 'latter' church wants to move away from. I had a first row view from the pew and saw it unfold. I have seen eyes rolled up when Mother slowly stands to sing her song. She may sing one of those old-time songs in her shaky voice that the younger members do not want to sing.

Although the Bible says in Titus 2:3-4, *"The aged women likewise, that they be in behaviour as becometh holiness, not false accusers, not given to much wine, teachers of good things; that they may teach the young women . . . to love their husbands, to love their children."* Older women are no longer free to instruct younger women because they are considered 'old fashioned' and not relevant in some of the 'latter' churches. Older men also are discouraged from leadership roles in the church. Many times they are relegated to the side pew without much acknowledgement or recognition.

No matter how long you've been a member of some of the 'family' churches, always remember, it is not 'your' church. You are just a guest that the ruling family has received and welcomes for a time. We should all be welcomed into the church like a brother or sister. When we are born again, everyone is a spiritual relative and should be treated as such. However, I have experienced the opposite often happens in some family churches. People who have been members of a church for many, many years after putting blood, sweat and tears into the church and its upkeep, but may come to find the church was never really theirs. The church 'belongs' to the pastor and his family.

In comparison to the large Catholic Church, which is run by the diocese of the Catholic bishops and headships, no one pastor 'owns' a Catholic church. Even in some Methodist, Baptist, and other denominations' churches, the pastor is sent there for a time to minister and he may be transferred somewhere else. In the independent black Pentecostal church, a pastor starts the church, owns the church and will run the church as he sees fit. So even by you joining and helping the church to thrive, it does not make it 'your' church.

I keep reiterating this fact because I've seen older people extremely hurt, and a few have died in pain, when the church they had attended for so many years asked them to leave because the church is going in a different direction. The poor senior church member feels too old to start over in a new church, and hurt because the people they know and love would just cast them aside.

Also, what I have seen happen in some 'family' churches, I find most disheartening, is a kind of last will and testament from some pastors; passing his position down to his son, who may or may not be able to pastor a church. Why can't the next pastor be the deacon's son, or the sister who may be called by God to pastor? Some Pentecostal pastors feel, because they started the church from the ground up and nourished and brought the church up to where it is today, the church should be passed down to his wife, who may be co-pastoring, or a son. The church is not a kingdom where the throne is inherited by the son. The church is the House of Prayer, and anyone God calls is well able to run the church; whether the new pastor be the son, daughter or the church mother's grandson.

I will explain how the church is treated like a kingdom. The children often inherit the throne from the pastor. Remember, this is just my lay person's view from the pew. Some people in leadership consider the church their personal kingdom. The pastor is king, his wife the queen, and the children are the prince and princess. When he can no longer rule the kingdom, his son is crowned king to carry on the hierarchy. No matter how hard and how long the servants may have worked to help build the kingdom, they will remain servants and serve the son who is the new king. In other words, the leader feels the church belongs to him because, after all, if it wasn't for his initiative to open the church, and if it wasn't for his gift to preach or sing, the church wouldn't be there. It was his hands that hewed the church from nothing to what it is today.

I heard one pastor say, "Nobody is going to tell me how to run *my* church!" All the members are his, the building is his, and all the money generated from the church belongs to him. Congregants must keep in mind the church is never 'your' church. It doesn't matter how long you've been a member or how much money you have put into it; in some 'family' churches, you are just a regular visitor where the ruling family allows you to come in to worship.

To go a step further, when people 'own' the church, they will name the church after themselves. Therefore, this brings up another issue we might wish to look at: are the names we give our churches appropriate or is it no big deal? Many people name their churches from Scripture—even though the names can be confusing in attempting to figure out what denomination the church is—such as John the Baptist Pentecostal Church. The Pentecostal Church names can be very, very long, and rambling. Also some churches are named after a current or past pastor or bishop. I, personally, find it troubling when pastors name the church after themselves. In recent times, people have even named ministries after themselves.

As I said earlier, the denominations are taken out of the names of some 'latter' churches and replaced with the word 'Center.' The church may be named the 'Lowly Bar Christian Center' under the auspices of Reverend Sadness. No one knows the denomination of the church. The organized churches, like those within the Baptist, Methodist, or Episcopalian faiths, require the denomination be noted in the names of their churches.

There are pastors, still alive, who have named their churches after themselves because they want it known it's their ministry and the ministry belongs to them! The church's name was changed from 'Our Lord's Pentecostal Church' to 'Williamson's Ministries.' Is it wrong to have family churches? Is it wrong to name churches after oneself? The answer for us pew-viewers is to seriously consider these issues.

The church is God's House of Prayer, of course, but in some 'family' churches, God's house is leased by the pastor's family. You, as a member in some 'family' churches, must pray the Lord sees your unselfish work and rewards you in Heaven. Everything you do, do it unto God. Do not do the work to be recognized and rewarded by your pastor or members of the church. Do not seek to have an anniversary every year to commemorate your good works in the church. Can we talk about the way we treat seniors in the church? Can we discuss whether or not church should be a hierarchy? Let's discuss.

| CHAPTER 12 |

The Church Is Not a Welfare Center

Here in America, we are fortunate to have government programs in place to help the poor. The elderly in other countries do not have support systems to assist the poor with their medical and physical needs. If the elderly do not have families to help them, they are mostly discarded like trash. Although we in America have social services, medical coverage and affordable housing to keep people from languishing in the streets, these programs can also make some people dependent on these services. If the young and poor do not have the ambition and drive to do better in life, they might accept the fate of their parents for themselves and lay around waiting for the monthly check and food stamps to arrive. So dependent are they on this income that they refer to it as 'my check,' as if they worked for it. I can talk about this mindset because I had this very same thinking when I was a young mother with three children, living in the projects of the Bronx. My thinking at that time was I have to sign up for social services because my husband walked out on me, now I'm left with three children to support.

Looking at the world with grey-colored glasses, I saw people as rich or poor. When I was a child, we were on welfare until my mother left New York City and moved to Miami. She took a job as a maid, cleaning white people's homes, and married my stepfather who was a worker in a bakery. When I grew up and married, I was so enchanted with the idea of having a husband, I did not consider what would happen if he stopped supporting me, stopped loving me enough through hard times, or ceased to have the integrity and dignity to support his own children.

When you have been poor for as long as I have been poor, you believe nice rich people will give you things. You believe the nice rich people will give you clothes they don't want, or food they don't need. Down through the years, this happened all the time, so I believed if I ask, they will give. I remember, back in the 1960s, when the social workers came to our apartment in the projects. As a young girl, I saw them go through each room and write down what my mother needed. She needed bunk beds for us, a washing machine, winter coats, and shoes. A few days later, my mother received an extra check and she was commanded to buy these things. The social workers would come back to our apartment to check and see if all these things were bought.

As social services tightened up their pocket strings, we were prone to borrow from people. The act of borrowing and begging became a part of me. Even into adulthood with my three children, I borrowed and I tried to make ends meet. How many people know that ends never meet? I borrowed from Peter to pay Paul until I found myself wallowing in despair. Now, I said all that to say this, after I received Christ into my life and joined a church, I came to church with this kind of begging and borrowing mindset. Many people are at this stage in their lives when they attend church. Thus, they see the church as another social service office.

Our Lord and Savior saw the people following Him, also, just for the loaves. I might add, they followed Him just for the bread. John 6:26 & 27 reads: *"Jesus answered them and said, Verily, verily, I say unto you, Ye seek me, not because ye saw the miracles, but because ye did eat of the loaves, and were filled. Labour not for the meat which perisheth, but for that meat which endureth unto everlasting life, which the Son of man shall give unto you: for him hath God the Father sealed."* Coming to church just to get financial assistance is not right. Sacrifice and budget to get to church in order to hear the Word of God, so you may grow thereby.

There was a time in the early 1980s that the black Pentecostal church went through what I call the 'Name It and Claim It' and 'Nab It and Grab It' phase. It was thought then that the reason we were poor and did not have much was because we did not have enough faith. So many messages came across the sacred desk of how we should name it and claim it. We took John 14:14, *"If ye shall ask any thing in my name, I will do it"*, and we ran with it. People were laying claim to very expensive Cadillac cars they could not make the payments on, while still living in the projects. Others were claiming houses they could not pay the mortgage for and testified how they were blessed to get those homes, only soon to be foreclosed on.

In order to acquire the things they were nabbing and grabbing, they forget to count up the costs. First, you have to qualify for these things, therefore, you need a good paying job to keep up with the payments. Why would you want a real expensive car with a huge car note, when you can barely afford to pay your rent in the projects? Why would you purchase a big house, with no down payment, when your income would not allow you to pay the rent for the apartment you have now? Your rent in the projects does not require you to also pay light, gas, insurance, oil to heat the house, and property taxes in addition to the mortgage. In my case, I was approved for credit to buy a floor model color television, bicycles for my children, wall-to-wall carpeting for my apartment in the projects; I even had gold venetian blinds put up on all the windows! I thought I was truly blessed until I couldn't keep up with the payments and my poor little paycheck was garnisheed! Talk about being distraught!

It's not that the Lord does not want us to have these things. He said in 3 John 1:2, *"Beloved, I wish above all things that thou mayest prosper and be in health, even as thy soul prospereth."* What we needed was our soul to prosper while we obtained these things. If we were filling our hearts and minds with the Word of God, we would have had the knowledge and wisdom of how to obtain and handle riches. We needed to know what to ask God for. When we ask Him for anything, we need to know the reason we are asking Him for it. We first needed to learn how to handle our finances. Can we save money and let it grow? Can we put aside forty dollars a month and not touch it, or do we spend it on some frivolous item like a bracelet or shoes we do not need? Are we faithful in paying our tithes to the church? Are we content in whatsoever state we find ourselves, or are we always dissatisfied and want to dress better than Sister Jones or have a bigger car than Brother Johnson? Haggai 1:6 reads: *"Ye have sown much, and bring in little; ye eat, but ye have not enough; ye drink, but ye are not filled with drink; ye clothe you, but there is none warm; and he that earneth wages earneth wages to put it into a bag with holes."*

It was not until I was taught the Word of God adequately that I stopped thinking in the manner of being poor and constantly needing help. I know now that my God is a miracle-working God. Once I obeyed the Word and started paying tithes, and giving what I could, I saw the increase of blessings in my life. Once I got off my dependency of begging my mother for help to buy Pampers, begging my neighbors for a cup of sugar, or borrowing ten dollars until pay day; only then did I see my life improve. Once I saw a way out by getting a job, a job with opportunities to move up the career ladder, I was then motivated to reach for higher goals. My children were enrolled into day care, and I felt good being able to support them, eventually, on my own.

Many, many people have not reached the independent mindset yet, and so they come to church constantly begging for money to pay light bills, rent or even to buy food and clothing. The church administrators do not want to be caught not fulfilling Matthew 25:35: *"For I was an hungred, and ye gave me meat: I was thirsty, and ye gave me drink: I was a stranger, and ye took me in."* The church wants to show hospitality and love, however, some church pastors and administrators will become exhausted and say to the person asking for help, "The church is not a welfare center!"

In the black Pentecostal church, I have seen people lined up at the pastor's office door after services waiting for carfare to go home. Other times, I have seen pastors standing outside the church door to pay a cab for a member who couldn't otherwise come to church. People claiming to not have two dollars and fifty cents to catch the bus to come to church. Why is the church obligated to pay the bills of its members, when the Word of God says in Philippians 4:19, *"But my God shall supply all your need according to his riches in glory by Christ Jesus."*

My view from the pew shows me some people will not sacrifice or put themselves out to attend church. Some people will buy what they want and rely on the church to pick up the slack. Some people will go anyplace they desire to go, but when it comes to church they want pickup and delivery service, or gas money. Some people are swallowed up in this world system by continuing to borrow from the "Pay Day Loan" outlets; which attach such high fees to the loans, people are obligated to hand over most of their paychecks in order to pay the loans off. This leaves them high and dry, financially, and they really cannot afford to come to church.

When you really desire to be in a prayer service, you will press your way to get there. Not praising myself, but I remember when I was half on welfare and working full time, I saved my subway fare for work and church. I pushed my baby carriages down to the church on the subway, and pushed my baby carriages back uptown on the subway to come home. Let's go back even further. My mother remembers a time when her grandparents, in the back woods of Sumter, South Carolina, rode for miles on a wagon driven by a mule to get to the old wooden church. Today we can live less than ten blocks from the church and still require a taxicab to get there?

To overcome this 'I am so poor' mentality, we need restoration of the mind. In order to obtain that restoration, we need to pray and allow the Bible to teach us how to be restored. The Holy Ghost is a comforter, and I am here to tell you He will lead and guide you. You will be surprised how your life will change for the better when you seek for the Holy Ghost. Doors will open that no man can shut. Opportunities will come forth that you never even thought of. By the grace of God, you will be able to budget your money, pay your bills, and depend on God and not the welfare system.

Desiring foolish things all the time will vanish and you will gain knowledge and the desire to buy what you need and only what you need. I know these thoughts will dissipate because you will not be so depressed. Depression has people shopping for gold necklaces, gold bracelets, widescreen televisions, the latest sneakers, anything they think will make them happy. Only to find out material things do not bring happiness. The love of God filling that emptiness in your heart will bring happiness and contentment. The desire to spend your hard-earned money on foolish things will end.

As you grow in the knowledge of God, you will advance in your career and in your life as you become a more devoted Christian. As the Bible states in Deuteronomy 28:12, *"The LORD shall open unto thee his good treasure, the heaven to give the rain unto thy land in his season, and to bless all the work of thine hand: and thou shalt lend unto many nations, and thou shalt not borrow."*

| CHAPTER 13 |

Offering

Perhaps people freely gave to the Disciples' missions, but no one was overburdened in giving. Also, the Disciples were not living in extravagance while the people scraped by. Jesus said in Matthew 22:21, *'Give unto Caesar what is Caesar's and unto God what is God's'*. I said earlier, I remember when pastors came out in a snow storm to bring food to the congregants. Of course, these days, this is missionary work and not a pastor's job. Alas, in the huge mega-churches, your pastor may not even know you! But if your need is made known, the missionary department of the mega-church may send someone out to your home to bring some support.

Some of the small black Pentecostal churches become overburdened and overwrought with requests for offerings, in addition to the regular offerings, tithes and mission obligations. The congregation is asked to contribute to the pastor's aid, pastor's anniversary, pastor's vacation, pastor's birthday, pastor's wife's birthday, and the pastor's salary, if the pastor is a full-time pastor. As a result, members are no longer joyful in giving in a free-will offering; instead, giving becomes a bone of contention and a burden.

The missionary offering, the one offering I feel is the most important of them all, which helps the community at large, is decreased in order for the church to handle the obligations of taking care of the pastor and his family. This chapter of the book will highlight the act of giving, which is another whole segment of church worship that has been hijacked by greed in some of the Pentecostal churches.

Due to the need of the leadership of the church to be on television, radio and to produce CDs and DVDs, money has become the main reason for running a church. Even if the church manages to have a radio broadcast, the pastor spends most of the time on the air pleading for money to stay on the air to plead for more money to stay on the air. Most of the small black Pentecostal churches cannot afford these expensive media outlets. However, saying this out loud may reveal we have little faith.

Back in the day, giving money in the church was the most stress-free part of worship. I remember when the bucket was placed on the offering table and people marched up, some even danced up to the table and dropped whatever amount they had to give: a dollar, a quarter, five dollars, whatever, while singing "Give, Give, Give, Give It in Jesus's Name." Paying tithes was and still is only ten percent of your income, which we are required to give.

Today, giving your offering has become a mind-boggling spectacle. People are swindled out of their money like never before. In the mega-church, to sufficiently fund the church, without passing buckets around where handlers were known to steal some of the money, the money is taken at the doors when the congregants walk into the church, like in the movie theatres at ticket booths. The money you give at the door is your offering for the day. Attempting to lift an offering from these great masses of people, streaming into the arenas, result in massive amounts of money that must be secured.

Some of the black Pentecostal churches of today use new words to encourage members to give. Formerly called giving a sacrificial offering or giving out of your need in order to receive a bigger blessing, is now called sowing a seed! If you sow a lot more seeds, you will reap a bigger harvest. Some of the larger churches have conveniently placed ATMs in the lobby so people can run out and get more money to give. Give until it hurts.

In 2 Corinthians 9:7, it reads: *"Every man according as he purposeth in his heart, so let him give; not grudgingly, or of necessity: for God loveth a cheerful giver.* Jesus loves a cheerful giver. If you are not cheerful when you give, but rather worried, stressed and anxious because you know if something don't turn around, your lights will be cut off, your car will be repossessed, or you will be evicted, don't give. Don't give under stress and duress, because the Lord loves a cheerful giver. Don't give out of boastfulness, either; because the Lord hates even a proud look (Proverbs 6:17). People marching up to the front of the church and making an announcement of the seeds they are sowing have already received their reward.

In Mark 12:44, Jesus saw all the givers at offering time giving out of their wealth, and noticed the little widow's mite. She only had two cents. The Lord noted that because she gave all she had, she gave more than everybody else. That reminds me of the rich, young ruler who thought by obeying the commandments he was doing all that was required of him. The Lord told him to sell all that he had and give to the poor, and then come and follow Him. The rich, young ruler went away sad because he could not do it. We give cheerfully when we know we have more money in the bank and we do not have to worry about our bills being paid. But giving when you are struggling, and doing so cheerfully and with full faith in God, well, that's a different story. Perhaps there may be big givers in the mega-churches who give silently. I'm sure some have given large sums of money and didn't want it announced.

Going back to the 'former' Pentecostal Church, the offering was lifted and the deacons prayed over it and then went to the back with the money, and the church service moved on to the next part of worship. Now, in the 'latter' Pentecostal Church, the money is lifted and counted right in front of the congregation and the total announced. If it is not up to the expectation of the deacon, a request for more money is asked of the congregation. Worse, there may be three or four offerings requested in the same service: one bucket for the church, another for the missionaries and another for pastor's aid. Then before dismissal, alas, another offering is collected for the speaker of the hour.

There was a very disturbing period in the Pentecostal Church; I think it started in the 1970s or 1980s, when at offering time, ministers started asking for $10 lines and $20 lines. If you wanted a big, supernatural blessing there were the $100 lines. Just imagine God doling out blessings according to how much money you can give. Oh, Father, forgive us for we know not what we do. This was a way to be seen giving in front of folks who may not have that much to give. Then, after all the 'special-blessing folks' finished giving, the minister might say, "OK, everybody else put whatever you have in your hands and come on up." In other words, you may not get that real special blessing the people with money will receive, but you might get something thrown your way if you give what you have. I do not believe the Lord is pleased with these gimmicks in getting people to give more money in the offerings. Perhaps the people giving whatever they have might receive that big, special blessing from the Lord like the little widow with the two mites. Maybe we could come together and discuss this issue and seek God's guidance in this also.

I was told, I do not know for sure, that some ministers plant three people in the audience with hundred dollar bills at offering time. The minister might say, "There are seven people in this place right now that can give a sacrificial offering of one hundred dollars!" Slowly, the three people stand up one by one. This may motivate others to sacrifice one hundred dollars. This will go on until seven people or more in the church stand holding a hundred dollars in their hands. Some people really do not have it to give, but in order to participate they will stand and give what we call a 'faith check.' That's a check that may bounce if the person cannot get the funds into the bank before the check gets cashed. Lord, help us!

You may not believe this, but this really happened at more than one Pentecostal church I have visited. During the offering part of the service, the congregation was held 'hostage' until the offering came up to the expectation of the minister. I mean, doors were locked and no one could leave until the goal was reached. I could name the churches right here, but I won't do that. You can tell this has left an indelible mark in my mind. While we sat there, we were given a good tongue-lashing for stealing from the Lord, and holding back and not having enough faith in God to give more. So people gave what they could out of duress, and not cheerfully I might add. Matthew 21:13 says, *"My house shall be called the house of prayer; but ye have made it a den of thieves."*

Luke 6:38 reads: *"Give, and it shall be given unto you; good measure, pressed down, and shaken together, and running over, shall men give into your bosom. For with the same measure that ye mete withal it shall be measured to you again."* God knows if you are giving freely or stingily. He knows if you could give more but choose not to, and He knows if you are giving under duress. Give freely.

The lyric in a gospel song we used to sing says, "You can't beat God's giving," and it is so true. I remember a time when giving one dollar was a lot for me to give. Then giving five dollars was hard. Watching people place a twenty in the offering pan was astonishing to me. Then, I was able to give twenty dollars in an offering without going home broke. Give what you have and want to give, and you will be blessed to give more. If you have the faith to give more than you are really able to give, do it, if that's what you really desire to do. If you give what you want to give and what you are able to give, then giving will be stress-free.

I can only imagine the life that rich, young ruler would have had if he obeyed the Lord and gave all he had to the poor. His life would have been more fulfilling, purposeful and happier. Like the song says, "You can't beat God's giving!" He might have received more than he had in money or in other ways. He might have been more content and healthier. He probably ended up worrying about his money and how best to keep it. What an empty life.

Some ministers ask that you 'give out of your need.' I presume that meant to give all that you have left and have faith that God will provide. Now, I don't know if you are going to be too cheerful doing that, unless you are ready to either die or have faith in God that He will provide for you. In 1 Kings 17:18, the woman in the Bible story was ready to die because she only had a little oil and a little flour left to bake a cake for herself and her son. She was going to bake the last cake for herself and her son, and then prepare to die. The prophet asked the woman to bake him the cake first; then bake a cake for herself and her son. She gave to the man of God first, and as promised, she did not run out of oil and flour until the drought was over. Since she was prepared to die anyway, she was willing to give all that she had. She did not see a way out. She did what the man of God asked her to do, and since you can't beat God's giving, she was blessed thereafter.

I remember one instance in my own life when the Lord Himself spoke to me during my time of financial distress. I was living in the projects in the Bronx with three children. At that time, the New York City Housing Authority assessed your rent by your gross income. I attended church and gave my tithes and offerings and I considered myself blessed. My net income did not cover the rent, day care, babysitting expenses, and carfare. I was discouraged and took my whole paycheck and threw it on the couch in despair. I cried, asking God how am I supposed to live?

I went across the street to the store to buy dinner, and a lady standing next to me was humming a song to herself. I watched her for a minute or two, wishing I did not have to worry about my financial hardship. I will never forget this for as long as I live; the Lord spoke to my heart, "Don't worry, don't fear, have faith" and a calmness came over me. I then felt I could hum a song and relax. I bought my dinner, calmed down and stopped crying. There's always tomorrow; keep going forth and have faith.

Somehow I paid the rent that month; and, several years later, I moved out of the projects, moved several times, and now I own where I live. I do not remember what song I hummed that day, but the song that comes to my mind now is: *Because He lives, I can face tomorrow, Because He lives, all fear is gone; Because I know He holds the future, And life is worth the living, Just because He lives!*

Giving cheerfully because you want to give is the way God wants to receive a gift from you. Hallelujah, Amen! The Bible tells us to give liberally and without grudge. If congregants develop negative feelings because of the financial situation of the church, they are then considered by church leadership to be people of little faith, robbing God and not cheerful givers. People start to be filled with animosity and even anger at offering time, which is not the right frame of mind to give unto the Lord. I know the church needs money to exist, but I do not think the offering should be received from people who are under duress. Let's straighten this out, Church. Let's take the rackets and scams out of giving and allow the people to give whatever the Lord placed on their hearts to give.

| CHAPTER 14 |

Why So Many Churches?

I believe if the Lord called you to open a church, your church will grow with people of all ages. Not only will it grow, but it will expand where other ministries will spring forth from it. I may be wrong, someone will be sure to correct me—but to say the Lord called you to open a church and your church is located on the second floor of a three story building, where there is a church on the first floor, one in the basement, another one on the third floor, another church on the corner of your block, and one across the street; each church having less than a dozen members, and all these churches never going out into the community to reach souls or even fellowship with each other, is so sad.

There are so many churches concentrated in one area. People are renting out barber shops and beauty parlors on Sundays, and setting up churches in them. They call Brooklyn in New York City "the borough of churches" because you may count on one block, on both sides of the street, about ten churches! Why are all these churches scrunched up in one block, all preaching from one Bible, never fellowshipping with one another, and never going out into the community? I was told by a seasoned prayer warrior, who has gone on to be with the Lord, that maybe there are so many churches in one place because it shows God's mercy and love for the lost. Sinners have a wide selection of churches to go to and find Salvation.

Correct me if I'm wrong, I certainly don't mind being corrected. I think there are so many churches piled on top of each other, in every crack and crevice of buildings in the poorest neighborhoods, because the church has become a form of income. Many people want to be chief and have their own church. Most of these churches are non-denominational because they do not want to be under any rules or regulations. The small black Pentecostal church—free-standing, non-denominational, mainly 'family' churches, not associated with any organizational head with no board, no one to reign in the pastor if he or she should stray—is there because the pastor wants to be the head of his own church. Many interpret the Bible in their own way, and will not sit under any leadership who will not see things their way. If I'm wrong, I stand corrected.

How can you tell if you are in a church run by a ruler? Take notice when visiting other churches and your pastor is the guest speaker. If he introduces his church to the host congregation by saying, "I want all *my* people who belong to *my* church to stand." This is a way of showing the other church how many members he or she has. The pastor stands with pride at how wonderful a leader he must be because he has eight more people in his church than the host church. When the leader keeps referring to the members of his congregation as *my people* instead of God's people, beware!

When we are moved to open a church, maybe we should ask the Lord to help us to open a church where there is a dearth of churches. Lord, show me where the church could be the most advantageous to the community at large. Help us to open churches where we won't be swapping members from neighboring churches. Years ago, you needed a letter of introduction from a previous pastor before you were able to join a new church. Most often the new member left the old church in disgrace or in anger and would not ask for a letter of introduction before joining a new church. Our desire should be to reach new souls for Christ, not open our doors to recycled people who are church-hopping. If we pray, I believe, we will not open churches upstairs over another church, or around the corner, or even sharing the same church.

The Disciples went out into all the world and shared the Gospel, starting churches in other countries and territories. Are we afraid to move out of our neighborhoods? Is it too inconvenient for us to open a church where there is no church? Why are we opening a church? Is it to provide a career and income for ourselves? Or is it to win souls and to preach the Gospel of Jesus Christ? I wonder. Just my view from the pew, but I wonder.

| CHAPTER 15 |

The 'Don't Judge Me' Generation

The old ways the Pentecostal churches used to conduct worship services are being discontinued because young people see the new dances on television or hear the new songs on YouTube and want to bring them into the church. The songs are not necessarily gospel songs; some of the songs are about good attributes like determination, inspiration or optimism. If it sounds good and has the right words, the young people want to bring it into the church and perform a dance to the songs.

The choir is moving like pop artists on television, and singing like the latest hip hop artists. The songs are not necessarily praises to Our Lord and Savior Jesus Christ. The congregation may begin to move and dance in a way that was never done in a sanctuary before! So now, we are no longer moving from side to side, clapping our hands to "What a Friend We Have in Jesus," but rather bumping and jerking to today's songs that may or may not have the name Jesus in it.

If by chance an old gospel song slips into the service and the Spirit takes over and people feel the presence of the Lord, they are amazed and often say, "There's nothing like those old-time gospel songs." I say those old-time gospel songs were written by people who went through hell and high waters and the words came to life in the writers' hearts. The songs stood the test of time because they praised God for His mighty acts.

In the 'latter' church, for millennials, the music has to be slamming, and the praise dancers have to be dancing to a current hit song to hold their attention. If you are able to pry the earphones out of their ears of the millennials, maybe they will hear some words of wisdom and advice; even though they still have a way of tuning you out. Although the church has lightened up on a lot of its rules, the millennials are more susceptible to the varying norms of lifestyles that do not seem abominable to them.

Certainly, the church will be different from the way I came up in the 1960s. The Bible reads in Hebrews 10:25, *"Not forsaking the assembling of ourselves together, as the manner of some is; but exhorting one another: and so much the more, as ye see the day approaching."* The young people may attend church by way of technology. The millennials feel they do not need to be physically sitting in a church all the time. They do not see the necessity of attending church every single Sunday. They do not want to get up, get dressed, drive or walk down to the church to hear the pastor speak or the choir sing. They do not mind attending church if there is something special happening, like a program, wedding or special function. So, what will the House of Prayer be like for the millennials?

The millennial church does most of their communicating through social media. Instead of standing on the street corners handing out tracts, they witness through social media. Ask any one of them what a tract is and get ready for blank stares. The millennials are not walking around with a big Bible under their arms. The entire Holy Bible is on an app that they can click on and find what they are looking for at a moment's notice.

They love to praise God and they will praise Him openly and sincerely, anywhere. Their music is different from the church music we are used to hearing, but they do praise the Lord. To them, listening to gospel does not exclude them listening to all other types of music. They know what is right and what is wrong, and they will live holy with the help of the Holy Ghost. As we wanted to be different and set apart from the world, the younger people would rather assimilate and blend in with the rest of society as much as possible. They don't want to be set aside and be ostracized by the world.

The young people will sing songs of praise with half their hair shaved off, tattoos on their arms, braids, dreadlocks, mohawks, piercings, and cut up jeans. All over the world, they are willing to die for their beliefs. The young ministers preach the Word on the pulpit wearing jeans, sneakers and their shirt tails out. They also have no qualms about wearing chains, jewelry in their nose and ears. The women wear makeup and pants while preaching the Gospel; no hang ups at all. Compared to the 'former' church when women would never, ever think of wearing pants and especially on the pulpit; now, it is common to see women preaching while wearing pants. Women ministers are also wearing big, jangling earrings and a lot of makeup; which in the 'former' church, they would have been called Jezebel.

You can walk down the street and not be able to spot a Christian anywhere until they open their mouths, because the 'latter' Christians meld into the crowd. Young Christians are wearing baggy pants, hats on backwards and listening to rap music, and still are able to quote Scriptures and lead others to Christ because they can relate to each other. They will lead devotion on the pulpits, or stage, wearing tee shirts, ripped jeans and sneakers. So, does it really matter what we wear in the churches?

Instead of people coming into the church with a repentant heart, sincerely seeking to give up their old way of life and put the desires of their flesh under subjection; we find people want to join the church and *keep* their sinful ways of life. In fact, the Pentecostal Church does accept people as they are initially, but we pray that with the preaching and teaching of the Word of God, and the person receiving the power of the Holy Ghost, he or she would put away their sinful ways and become born again. We find not only do people not wish to give up their sinful lifestyles, in fact, they would go a step further and suggest the church revise its rules and standards to accommodate their sins.

Back in the days of the 'former' church, when someone was involved in sin, that person usually did not want to join a church because he was concerned about being a hypocrite. Members of the church would explain to the sinner that he did not need to wait until he stopped sinning to attend church; the church will work with him. I can remember when people would not even smoke a cigarette in front of a church. They held the church in such high esteem, they would put the bottle of liquor in their back pockets or hide the cigarette until they walked away from the doors of the church.

It is no surprise to many that the sinner knows the rules of the church and what the Bible says about sin. Romans 3:23 reads: *"For all have sinned, and come short of the glory of God."* These days, the enemy of our souls has convinced people, especially the ones in the small Pentecostal church, in desperate need to fill the empty pews that the church should water down its standards. Perhaps some of the sins people are committing should be tolerated in order to keep people in the pews. The enemy of our souls has convinced the church that it should not require people to change their lifestyles because, after all, we are all just flesh. On the contrary, the church must be careful not to be deceived into accepting sinful lifestyles. The constant refrain of the rebellious, the stiff-neck, and the bound is "Don't judge me!"

In St. John 8:4, the woman caught in the very act of adultery, the men were about to stone her to death. Jesus asked the accusers to throw the first stone if they had not sinned. None of them could throw that first stone. Then Jesus said to the woman, "Go thou and sin no more." This is where the rubber meets the road in the 'latter' church. If the woman was anything like some women of today, she might have required the church to prevent the people from coming against her, but still desired to continue being a sinner. She'd say, "Just don't judge me. I have a right to be or do whatever I want to be or do. So the church should accept me as I am." Should the church accept the sins because it does not wish to 'offend' the sinner? God forbid! Jesus said, *"Go, and sin no more."* Repent, because God has saved you from death!

| CHAPTER 16 |

Generation Gap

When speaking to people born in the 1980s and 1990s, born right in the middle of the great Pentecostal transition from 'former' to 'latter' church, I find their beliefs in the church are very different from those of my generation. During their childhood, the church had started loosening up its strict rules and regulations. The X and Y Generations are still young enough to remember the old rules of the church. This is the generation that demanded changes in the church. During their teenage years, the onset of pop songs sung by Michael Jackson, Whitney Houston and Mariah Carey were enticing and addictive. To add more enticement were the gospel singers of that time who were introducing songs that sounded very similar to the secular artists. These twenty- and thirty-year-olds were sitting in the church as children torn between the changes in the church that they demanded, while being keenly aware of the changes in the secular world. While they observed the church's loosening of the rules, and the popularity of Michael Jackson and other artists, they did not want to be too far removed from society. When many of them grew into adulthood, they decided to not be so stringent with their children regarding church rules and church attendance.

Compared to my generation of the 1950s and 1960s, who sat passively while the elders sang the old traditional worship songs, we sang and clapped along obediently in the church. We were told in no uncertain terms, we will not sing any of the songs made popular on television and radio. The X and Y Generations, in comparison, will not sit quietly and endure the long worship services of the 'former' church. They demanded change and if the change did not come, they were leaving the church. However, what evidently happened, the younger generation did not leave, they changed the church. Coincidentally, the children of the 1980s and 1990s defied almost all the old rules and stood steadfast in their mode of dress, presentation and, of course, their music.

The young boys want to wear their earrings, cornrows and jeans in the church, which, before the 1980s, I, as a pew-viewer, had never seen before. They want to change the music, and since most of the boys were the musicians of the church, they added hip hop beats to the church songs unbeknownst to most of the elders. Hebrews 12:14 reads: *"Follow peace with all men, and holiness, without which no man shall see the Lord."*

Now most of the children's children, the millennials, believe that living holy means to just be a good person. You do not need to adhere to complete separation from the world and all its lifestyles. The truth is, you cannot really live holy if you are not filled with the Holy Ghost. Therefore, the 'it-doesn't-take-all-that' generation will and has desecrated the church with all manner of dress, dances and music, which grieves the hearts of true, born again Christians.

These days, in the 'latter' church, a worship service is like attending a rock concert. Strobe lights are moving across the stage in different colors. The video screens on both sides of the pulpit cover every angle of the praise singers. The band plays the music loud and blaring, and there's even theatrical smoke coming up from the floor of the pulpit, or should I say stage, as the singers jump up and down to the beat. One of my relatives told me there was an incident where one of the praise singers choked from the stage smoke and had to be escorted off the stage!

The millennials are different from all previous generations. They are wise in technological and digital applications and equipment. This knowledge gives them the ability to make music and voices come alive and be clearer to the ear, as well as distort the sounds. This generation is bored easily and cannot concentrate on one thing very long. They can simultaneously text, listen to music and hear you speaking 'at' them. If they are not on the praise dance team, utilizing technical equipment or involved in the music ministry, then they have no use for church.

They desire to assimilate and be a part of things. They do not want to be different from their peers. I cannot say all millennials want to be like their peers, because I believe God has some who are living holy and Sanctified unto the Lord. Forget rules and regulations, forget dress codes, forget about listening to preachers for over two hours. They need sound, visual stimulations and, most of all, participation.

In the larger churches, the young people's church service is conducted separately from the adults to accommodate the dancing, singing and louder music. Lights! Camera! Action! If the church service is not a big production with entertainment, dancing and singing with spotlights and smoke, then you've lost most of the millennials.

In some of the 'latter' black Pentecostal churches, there is a definite large generation gap. The congregations are comprised mostly of the middle-aged to seniors, and then the very young children and babies. The Pentecostal Church, with its requirements for living holy and giving up the sins of this world, have very few teens and people in their twenties attending church on a consistent basis. If they do come, they come unmarried with children or living in a 'relationship.' They come wearing their jeans, tee shirts and sneakers. They come with their piercings, tattoos, and their hair done in a style that defies gravity.

A young person I know, who was born in 1998, told me she only attends church because she likes the music. Although she is in her late teens, she is still too young to have gone through much of life's ups and downs to really appreciate the real relevance of church and worshipping God. Surely, she will come to know the true meaning of praise and worship as she grows older. Like one of the older prayer warriors once told me, "If you haven't gone through many trials and tribulations, just keep on living."

This young person's life is full of pressures and major decisions she has to make on her own. If she decides to disobey her parents and grandparents and chooses not to attend church, she is also pressured by gender identification by her school administrators and classmates. If she becomes pregnant out of wedlock, her school will help procure medical coverage for abortions without the knowledge of her parents. The enemy of our souls is working overtime on this present generation because prayer and all things religious were taken out of the schools, giving him free range to push sin. By offering condoms, birth control pills, and enforcing the thinking that parents are wrong and the school administrators are right, the enemy is convincing the young that it's alright to sin.

Your young daughter can hemorrhage at the dinner table from a botched abortion, and you will not know what happened. In fact, your daughter could have had two or three abortions by the time she's seventeen, without your knowledge. Some might say better communication between the parents and the child could prevent this from happening. Let me say this, you can raise your child in the admonition of the Lord, but the enemy of our souls and his imps working through school administrators, peers and boyfriends can convince your daughter that what you are teaching is wrong. Because your child wants to assimilate and be 'like everybody else,' she may be deceived into thinking her friends' way of living is the right ways.

With the impact of technology, texting, sexting and bullying are common place now. So much so that young people showing their private parts on cell phones is all the rage. The young people are not ashamed or alarmed by it and will share these pictures all over the world. The ease with which people will subject themselves to be violated on social media is mainly due to some of the young people wanting to assimilate with peers and their rejection of the church. The more the parents live for Christ and pray against the enemy of our souls, the more the enemy fights us through our children. It appears the church's children seem to be the ones who are the most rebellious. The enemy uses them to fight you and your walk with God in his attempts to bring reproach to the church.

As I have stated before, the enemy of our souls is a liar and he cannot tell the truth. He lies to the children telling them what they are doing will not hurt them. That same lying wonder told Eve, "You shall not surely die," in Genesis 3:4. He is still lying today, telling the young people to disobey their parents and grandparents because the parents do not know what they are talking about; they're old fashioned. John 10:10 reads, *'The thief, comes to steal, to kill, and to destroy.'* He is a thief because he is stealing the lives of our young people; he is stealing their happiness, joy and carefree lives and destroying their future. I see the agenda of the enemy is to destroy the young people by contaminating their minds, killing them with violence and drugs, and leading them away from the church. I pray the Lord will keep them from the evil one. We must continue to pray and pray fervently for the children.

When this young girl attends church, if only to hear the music, she cannot receive the minister's instructions because she has already heard her principal, teachers, administrators, and school nurse tell her it is alright to sin and disobey your parents and the church. Your parents and grandparents read the Holy Bible, which some of the judges in our courts refer to as an 'ancient book' that should not be adhered to today. The 'ancient book' reads in 2 Timothy 4:3-4, *"For the time will come when they will not endure sound doctrine; but after their own lusts shall they heap to themselves teachers, having itching ears; And they shall turn away their ears from the truth, and shall be turned unto fables."*

While sitting on the pew and observing all these changes, it hurts so much. Our grandchildren are products of society instead of the church. Our own children wanted changes in the church, now *their* children are rejecting the church and its rules. Some of our children have joined gangs in order "to belong." Some have become teenage parents and dropped out of school because they believed a lie. St. Luke 16:8 reads: *"for the children of this world are in their generation wiser than the children of light."* The children of this world have convinced the children of light that they do not have to live all holy and Sanctified. They should do whatever they want to do. After doing all they were big enough to do, their lives are virtually destroyed. The young people become even more bitter and angry realizing their lives have become harder and more depressing.

Oh, by the way, did you know that the saying 'each generation is weaker and wiser' is not written in the Bible? That saying has been passed down by many people as a Bible verse. No, today's generation is not weaker, nor are they wiser. What they are is more confused because of the amount of information coming at them at such rapid pace. We must pray for our children as Jesus prayed for His followers in St. John

17:15, *"I pray not that thou shouldest take them out of the world, but that thou shouldest keep them from the evil."*

My desire is to have churches, the holy Pentecostal churches, be available and pure from the trappings of this world and at the ready to receive these souls in pure holiness when they come. We know if we do not pass the torch to the next generation, whatever you are involved in, it will soon become extinct. The smaller black Pentecostal church, where many congregations are devoid of teenagers, must return to the old landmark. While society is telling our young people it is OK to live vicariously—go ahead and party, drink, smoke, dabble in drugs, gamble, have sex outside of marriage—we older Christians know that the wages of sin is death (Romans 6:23).

The word most often used by people who feel doing a little sin here and there will bring no harm is "balance." Everything in life has to be balanced; too much of anything is not good. What does balance mean, biblically? It means stay on the fence. Revelation 3:16 reads: *"So then because thou art lukewarm, and neither cold nor hot, I will spue [spew] thee out of my mouth."* In other words, to be a true born again Christian, you should be wholly involved with your walk with God. You are either for or against. You can't be half in and half out. You are giving your whole life to Christ or not at all. Luke 16:13 reads: *"No servant can serve two masters: for either he will hate the one, and love the other; or else he will hold to the one, and despise the other. Ye cannot serve God and mammon."* That said, I believe—remember, I said "I believe"—that some of the 'latter' Pentecostal churches are trying to serve God and mammon.

The new modus operandi is: *"We have to keep the young people in the church."* Problem is, whatever you are doing to keep the young people, you will have to keep doing it. If you are building a skating rink on top of the church, the skating rink will have to remain there for the young people to stay. If you are leasing space down the block for a church 'night club,' which plays contemporary-to-temporary gospel music so that the young people can hang out as if they are at a real night club, you will have to keep that night club thing going. If the teenagers are having their own services in the basement of the church because they don't want to listen to the worship service their parents are having in the main sanctuary, well, you know what the results of that will be.

Hebrews 13:8 reads: *"Jesus Christ the same yesterday, and today, and forever."* Let me tell you a secret: what it took for Grandma to be saved, will take the same for the young people to be saved! Young people will have to bend those knees and cry out to the Lord for deliverance just like Grandma did. No club, skating rink or special 'young people' service will keep them in the days of trials and tribulations. There comes a time in everyone's life when they must endure sound doctrine in order to be able to endure bad situations and horrible times in life. When that time comes, they will not be looking for a club to run into; they will be looking for that tower, that's higher than I. If you do not believe me, keep on living. Proverbs 18:10 reads, *"The name of the LORD is a strong tower: the righteous runneth into it, and is safe."*

I wrote in my first book, *My Life at the World Trade Center*, how the Lord spared my life, twice, in both attacks on the towers. I remember President George W. Bush asking all churches to open their doors so that people may go in and pray. People filled the churches in the days following 9/11. People didn't seek out the bars, clubs, strip joints, or skating rinks; they sought the Lord for they knew where their help came from. The church must be the church at all times. The church must be strong and accessible with all the power of prayer at the ready. Am I right about it? Let's discuss!

| CHAPTER 17 |

O Zion, What's The Matter Now?

I guess you are saying by now, "For a person who claims she's not a preacher or holds any authority in the church, she sure uses a lot of Scriptures!" Scriptures just come to my mind on most topics automatically. If you sat in the church for over fifty years, the Word is etched in your heart and, in addition, after being filled with the Holy Spirit, the Scriptures come easily to your remembrance. If you live long enough and go through enough situations in life, you will become an authority on several issues. Because I am a professional pew-viewer, I see things going on in the church that disturb and vex my spirit. Therefore, I need to talk about it and bring issues up, so we can look at them and perhaps make corrections.

In 1 Corinthians 5: 1 -5, there is a story of a man who slept with his father's wife. Paul the apostle could not understand why the church allowed such an atrocity as that to go on and the church do nothing about it. Apostle Paul, astonished and bewildered, said this grievous sin was not even heard of in the wicked secular world. Even the sinners know sleeping with a father's wife is unthinkable. Paul reasoned the church was so puffed up that they did not even mourn such a sin.

Sin hasn't changed, but with technology, we hear and see it more graphically and openly, and at a faster rate. Some sins we never even heard of when we were growing up, because it may have been kept secret. Young people today are aware of all sorts of evil deeds going on in the world. 'Back in the day,' people didn't discuss certain dark secrets out in the open. Today, grievous sins are all over the television, the Internet and newspapers. It is broadcast all the time, all day long, until people become immune to most of it. After a while, people begin to accept some sins as normal. Even the people in the church don't mourn sins anymore. Just like the people in this story in Corinthians where the son slept with his father's wife, Apostle Paul was astonished the church did nothing about it.

I am astonished some in the Pentecostal Church no longer mourn the works of the flesh as told in Galatians 5:19-21, *"Now the works of the flesh are manifest, which are these; Adultery, fornication, uncleanness, lasciviousness, Idolatry, witchcraft, hatred, variance, emulations, wrath, strife, seditions, heresies, Envyings, murders, drunkenness, revellings, and such like . . . they which do such things shall not inherit the kingdom of God."* In the 'former' church, it was really shameful for a young girl to have a baby out of wedlock. In the 'former' black Pentecostal church, she was treated pretty much like the woman caught in the very act of adultery in the Bible, minus the stoning. The young girl would have to stand in front of the church and ask forgiveness of the congregation, then sit in the back of the church for the full term of her pregnancy, shaming her. The father of the baby would have to sit in the back of the church, too, if he showed up.

In addition, divorce and remarriage were prohibited. In the 'former' church, people lived celibate lives because they were not allowed to remarry until the spouse passed away. Nowadays, people put away wives and husbands like changing shirts. Remarrying has become so common—I recently visited a church that was once the strictest in church rules and regulations. For years, this large Pentecostal church's pastor and his wife of over thirty-odd years sat in the pulpit together. I visited this church a couple years ago, and the once strong, adamant Pentecostal pastor had a new, younger wife sitting in the pulpit with him. His first wife is still alive. Not judging him; this business is between him, his wives and God. However, I will ask, where does that leave the congregation? All that was taught to the congregation for years, is it now in question? Many more divorces and remarriages are occurring in the church. Divorce is so prevalent in churches today, many people are working on their second and third spouses. The result is so many children living in broken homes and instability.

Let's discuss right here the gravity of making a vow to God. I believe the excitement of having this big, white beautiful wedding with all the trimmings clouds the importance of making the wedding vow. As family and friends admire the bride's dress and the groom's tuxedo, the oohs and aahs of the guests admiring the flowers and the beautiful white stretch limousines, push the vows out of their thoughts. No matter if the pre-marriage counseling attended beforehand took hold in the minds of the marrying couple; the sight of the beautiful, sparkling diamond wedding ring captivates the minds, and the vows become just a small part of the ceremony. Truthfully, the vow is the most important part of the wedding ceremony. The vow is the whole reason for marrying in the first place.

It reads in Ecclesiastes 5:4-5, *"When thou vowest a vow unto God, defer not to pay it; for he hath no pleasure in fools; pay that which thou hast vowed. Better is it that thou shouldest not vow, than that thou shouldest vow and not pay."* As I sit at my view from the pew, I believe people do not know how very important what making a vow to God really means. Walking down the aisle, in the sanctuary of the Lord, standing before God's minister, making a vow before God and all present is significant. A person needs to pray and consider the weight of the vow before making it. If you are a person that is weak in the flesh, you should really consider the vow and the reason you are making that vow. Will you be able to keep the vow? If the sole purpose of you marrying is because you are burning in the flesh, and you really do not love the person you are marrying, then you should pray to bring your flesh under subjection. Marriage is not going to correct that problem for you; instead, you will be lusting after others while married.

The most common vow is the following: *"Do you take [Bride's/ Groom's name] to be your wedded [wife/husband], to live together in marriage? Do you promise to love her/him, comfort her/him, honor and keep her/him for better or worse, for richer or poorer, in sickness and health, and forsaking all others, be faithful only to her/him, for as long as you both shall live?"* You will not be faithful only to him or her when you are a very lustful person to begin with. When you love someone, you do not desire to hurt the person you are marrying in any way. When you abuse your wife physically and/or mentally, you have broken your vow. When you divorce your husband because he's not of the social standing you thought he should be, you broke your vow. When financial issues force you to leave your home, your vow has been broken. If the spouse commits all manner of evil deeds and brings sin into the marriage, the vow is broken.

What really concerns me are the ministers who perform the marriages of people he or she knows are entering the second or third marriage. I hate to think the minister officiated the previous marriage(s) and is now officiating over this one. There are ministers who ask no questions, who even know the previous wife or husband and is now introduced to the new intended.

Would it be essential for the ministers to ask to see divorce papers or death certificates, which might alleviate questions and verify the status of previous marriage(s)? In the 'latter' church, most of the pre-marriage certification and verification is not done. Sin has prevailed so much in the church, even the minister's marriage(s) may be in question. Believe it or not, there are people who are not even divorced from their present spouse, walking down the aisle of the church getting married. This is not only illegal, it is also immoral; but it is happening.

Walking down the aisle again and again to make the same vow to the Lord becomes a lie. Psalms 101:7 reads: *"He that worketh deceit shall not dwell within my house: he that telleth lies shall not tarry in my sight."* Since we know that a liar will not even tarry in God's sight, I wonder if his vow at the altar is even heard by God. If we as born again Christians would treat our spouses with love, respect, honor, and kindness, I'm sure there would be fewer divorces in the church.

From my view from the pew, I see there are many people in the church who refuse to deny the flesh. The biggest mistake we make is falling into temptation, believing we are missing out on something. The enemy of our souls tells us that the other woman or man is what we can have. Your wife or husband is getting old and, after all, you still have needs. Then we bite, go against the vow we made to the Lord, and divorce the spouse and leave our children.

The Bible reads in Matthew 16:24, *"Then said Jesus unto His disciples, 'If any man will come after me, let him deny himself, and take up his cross, and follow Me."* There is a cross we have to bear. It will not be easy. It's a trial we can win the victory over if we trust in the Lord and follow Him. The old gospel song says:

> *"Must Jesus bear the cross alone,*
> *and all the world go free?*
> *No, there's a cross for everyone*
> *and there's a cross for me."*

I believe all these bad situations exist in the church today because we have let the standards slip. We, the children of God, will not stand up like Paul and say, *"Yes, I will judge!"* Apostle Paul said in 1 Corinthians 5:3-5, *"I'm not even there with you, but I will judge and with the Lord Jesus Christ, I cast such a person away"* The sinner who slept with his father's wife was still sitting in the pews as if he's done nothing wrong. We often say, "Oh, we can't cast people out of the church today; what about the parable of the wheat and the tares growing together?" Matthew 13:30 reads: *"Let both grow together until the harvest: and in the time of harvest I will say to the reapers, Gather ye together first the tares, and bind them in bundles to burn them: but gather the wheat into my barn."* Some people might say, casting people away for doing grievous sins would be mean. God said we must show love. Don't judge. Paraphrasing Paul, "I am not there in person, but just hearing about this grievous sin makes me stand in righteous indignation and say, 'No, this is wrong!'"

Listen, Church, the enemy of our souls knows his time is not long. Like I said earlier, I am not a minister so I will not try to interpret Scripture. I just would like us to think about how best to handle the onslaught of blatant sins in the church. Should we tolerate it or pray against it? The enemy hates God and the Devil hates you, too. St. John 10:10 says, *"The enemy comes to steal, kill and to destroy.* He's not playing, and we cannot afford to play around with him either! We have power with God, and we have power to stand up and plead the blood against the enemy.

Today, many are coming into the church without a repentant heart. We pray for willing hearts that want to repent and follow the Lord. In the 'latter' church, it seems we do not want to offend anyone. Back in the day, the older members showed love but at the same time they told you the truth. They did not sugarcoat anything about your soul's Salvation. These days, the older members do not want to hurt anyone's feelings, thus, a lot of sin is prevalent in the church. We know of the sins, and we know it is not right, but we tolerate it. Some of the younger members do not see the harm. They feel people are people, and everyone should live and let live. The phrase the young people like to use is, "It's not that serious!" It is very serious! Where people will spend eternity is at stake! The 'latter' church may feel as long as the sinners are consenting adults, and not hurting anybody, leave them alone.

People have stood in church, having dumped their spouses and families for a younger, more attractive partner pleading, "I ask for forgiveness and I apologize to my family. Please give us our privacy." The Bible reads in 2 Corinthians 5:21, *"For he hath made him to be sin for us, who knew no sin; that we might be made the righteousness of God in him."* Jesus died to take away the sins of the world. We can come boldly to the throne through the blood of Our Lord and Savior Jesus Christ and seek Salvation. The church should be praying for souls that want to cast off this world and follow Jesus and not be hard-hearted, stiff-necked sinners, desiring to come into the church with their sins and to remain the same.

With the people becoming more emboldened to stay in their sins while attending church, along with the church's lowered standards, not willing to pray that the Lord help them to live consecrated and Sanctified lives, allows even more grievous sins to be accepted into the church. My generation, the Baby Boomers, is undoubtedly getting older and dying out. I do not know what my mother's generation is called. The black Pentecostals of her generation are the prayer warriors that came up out of the Jim Crow, deep segregated south. They are the consecrated, Sanctified saints of the Most High who didn't tolerate sin in any way, shape or form, much less allow it to permeate the church. They are the seniors of the church that no one wants to listen to anymore. What will happen to the Pentecostal Church after we are gone? Will there still be a church as we know it? Will there still be people holding up the blood-stained banner, preaching holiness, seeking the power of the Holy Ghost, and being a light in this dark and evil world? I certainly hope so.

EPILOGUE

Let Us Hear the Conclusion of the Whole Matter (Ecclesiastes 12:13)

Now that we have discussed the 'former' and 'latter' states of the black Pentecostal church—granted, as I see it—what should we do about it? My point of view from the pew is definitely slanted toward keeping the church traditional, a sacred place for prayer and meditation. This might be boring to the younger generation, but the church should be the place to go when people want to pray and have the Lord speak to their hearts and minds.

Perhaps what we wear to church or the music we listen to may or may not be that important. Perhaps it is irrelevant the style in which we wear our hair or the jewelry we wear. Maybe the distinction that we dance in the Spirit or in the flesh is not that important. All these concerns might not be such major issues. In comparison to the real, horrid events going on in the world today, concerns about hairstyles and clothes may not be that important. Maybe these concerns are just old folks' worries.

Some of the old rules could have been placed in the church by the elder members just to see if we would be obedient. Then again, maybe there are some restrictions we should abide by according to Scripture because the Lord requires holiness. Let the inward beauty show through, rather than all the shiny and fancy apparel. Let us adorn ourselves with sobriety. Let people see you and not all the elaborate, extravagant, even outrageous apparel. 1 Peter 3:4 reads, *"But let it be the hidden man of the heart, in that which is not corruptible, even the ornament of a meek and quiet spirit, which is in the sight of God of great price."* Our choirs, ministers and lay members should not wear revealing clothes. It hurts me to see great gospel artists singing about Our Lord and Savior Jesus Christ with gowns cut down to the stomach revealing cleavage. If you are hurt by it, shouldn't we talk about it? Let's discuss. Let's teach our young how to dress according to holiness.

The House of Prayer does not have to be elaborate, in my opinion, with very expensive and gaudy chandeliers and thick carpeting. Yes, the Lord should have the best, but I believe the Lord wants His house to be a place anyone can walk into and receive Salvation. Others may feel the church should move with the times and 'upgrade' to a much more modern church. The modern church should not only have chandeliers and thick carpeting, but also colorful strobe lights, video screens, cameras, cushiony plush seating, children's church, a nursery, main sanctuary, the overflow rooms, offices, security guards, security clearances, and massive beautiful pulpits that wrap around the front of the church with yards and yards of carpeting on it, with only a plant and a podium placed at its center.

Nowadays, we change the vernacular for 'church worship' and call it 'church experience.' Oh, how I hate to hear that term describing church services. "How was your 'church experience' this Sunday? Was it working for you?" It sounds as if we should expect a 'thrill' when attending church. Instead, church worship should be a soul-saving, life-changing, renewal with Christ. After you receive Salvation, each time you enter into church, it does not become an experience, but a resurgence of spiritual growth and renewing of the mind. Using the word 'experience' sounds temporary; Salvation and being born again are permanent!

We see that the 'latter' church has surpassed the 'former' church, with new technologies and advancements in education. Often, for real spirituality, the 'latter' church has to reach back to the 'former' church for relevance and wisdom. In these current times, our songs have to be much more comprehensive and less haphazard. The music instruments are enhanced and digitized, thus, allowing the praise and worship to change from the old washboard and bass drum sound to more sophisticated and intricate sound.

The 'former' church songs have what we call the anointing and people can feel the Spirit moving when the songs are sung. On the other hand, we no longer wallow in the sawdust, crying and wailing for change to come. Change has come; perhaps too much change has come to the Pentecostal church, so much so, the church has lost its purpose and its convictions.

There are plenty of theatres, arenas, clubs, and amusement parks people can go to without the church attempting to attract people in that fashion. Believe me, when people are ready to finally come over to the Lord, after the enemy of our souls has beaten them down, they will come. They will come looking for a church, a real House of Prayer. I pray there will still be true Pentecostal churches around to receive the wayward and the lost.

This discussion, essentially for the 'former' Pentecostal Church pew-viewers, leaves me in an almost similar situation as the Prophet Elijah. I said to myself, "Well, this is the new church, get used to it. Our old ways of worship are dead." 1 Kings 19:9 reads, *Then he [Elijah] came thither unto a cave, and lodged there; and, behold, the word of the LORD came to him, and he said to him, What doest thou here, Elijah?"* I ask the same question to the 'former' Pentecostal Church, what are we doing here? Do we really have good reason to believe the Pentecostal Church as we knew it is dead?

In the story, Elijah answers the Lord in verse 10: *"I have been very zealous for the LORD God of hosts: for the children of Israel have forsaken thy covenant, thrown down thine altars, and slain thy prophets with the sword; and I, even I only, am left; and they seek my life, to take it away."* In Romans 11:3-5, the Lord responded, *"I have reserved to myself seven thousand men, who have not bowed the knee to the image of Baal. Even so then at this present time also there is a remnant according the election of grace."* The answer for us today is, no, the black Pentecostal church is not dying. Our God will always have a remnant. I take heart in knowing there are churches that have not left the foundation of its faith. All Pentecostal churches have not been modernized to suit the 'microwave' generation. There are still Pentecostal ministers who will not rush through the services and are indeed taking the time needed to minister to the people.

Very recently I visited a 'latter' Pentecostal church, and I am so happy (and relieved) to report that the church is still alive and well. I was like Elijah, until the Lord let me see that He has many Pentecostal churches that have not bowed down to the pressures of society. There are many pastors who are unafraid to cry out and spare not His Word. I'm just one person and therefore cannot attend every Pentecostal church, so I am sure there are many Pentecostal churches out there I will never know about. I have visited Pentecostal ministries where the edict of the church is not eliminated or compromised.

I walked into one particular Pentecostal church one Sunday in the Bronx, where the people were dancing, singing and praising the Lord. The lights were on, heads were lifted up and hands raised in adulation, worshipping and praising our God. The organist was playing the organ, the drummer was hitting those drums, and the songs of Zion were sung high and powerful. There were a couple of flat screens on the walls, but no one was standing around staring at the screens, because everyone was too busy praising the Lord. The music from the worship service could be heard from the streets as you entered into the sanctuary. And, get ready for this, the praise and worship service lasted for over an hour!

Some of the people in the church did not sit in their seats the entire praise and worship portion of the service. This, I have not seen in a long time! All over the sanctuary people were crying, praising God, dancing, and worshipping God with all their might. I myself could not keep looking around because, as the 'latter' church young people say, "I had to get my praise on, too!" All the praise songs, new ones and old ones, were warning the enemy of our souls, in no uncertain terms, that he is defeated.

The pastor's sermon left no holds barred, either. The young, dynamic pastor was on fire for God. He touched on current events and intertwined present day problems with Bible truths that went straight at the heart of the people. He cried loud and spared not, unflinchingly departing the Word of God with meaning and understanding (Isaiah

58:1). He spoke to the young and old, relating to the needs of all generations.

Today, people realize they need a deeper relationship with God; a God who can change their lives for the better. They realize their need to be made whole in every aspect of their lives. As the old gospel song goes:

> *"Search me, O God,*
> *And know my heart today;*
> *Try me, O Savior,*
> *Know my thoughts, I pray.*
> *See if there be some wicked way in me;*
> *Cleanse me from every sin, and set me free."*

I want to possess the fruit of the Spirit in Galatians 5:22-26 - *"which is love, joy, peace, longsuffering, gentleness, goodness, faith, Meekness, temperance: against such there is no law. And they that are Christ's have crucified the flesh with the affections and lusts. If we live in the Spirit, let us also walk in the Spirit. Let us not be desirous of vain glory, provoking one another, envying one another."* The black Pentecostal church will continue to be a House of Prayer if it continues in the faith and true holiness. The Scripture I used for this book, Haggai 2:9, reads: *"The glory of this latter house shall be greater than of the former, saith the LORD of hosts: and in this place will I give peace, saith the LORD of hosts."*

ACKNOWLEDGMENTS

I could not have written this book without the guidance of my Lord and Savior Jesus Christ. Thank you to all my family, friends and loved ones who gave me their opinions and experiences as members of the church. These associate pew-viewers love and support their churches all over the country and desire the church to remain that beacon of hope. I know many of you will uphold our church leaders in prayer. A heartfelt thanks to my mother, Rev. Dr. Ruth D. Singletary, who is my pastor, and she has raised her five little children in the church. She even taught us how to sing and called us the "The Holy Five". With joy and gratitude, I would like to thank some of the pastors (some have gone on to be with the Lord), who prayed and taught me the Word of God down through the years: Bishop Elnora Smith, Pastor Edna Sheffield, Pastor Thomas McCamery, Bishop Clarence E.S. Jones, and Rev. Dr. Ruth Singletary. As a member of the Prayer Band during the 1980s and 1990s, praying for so many in schools, nursing homes, hospitals, homes, prisons, and churches, thanks to all of them: Lydia Stowers, Liza M. Williams, Elnora Smith, Ada McCollough, Josephine Wright (deceased), Mother Ida McPhatter and Elder Odell Stowers. A very special thanks to my friends who contributed to this book: Leslie Wong Scott and Loraine Sherod. I want to thank and acknowledge Pastor Yurvette Maxfield of New Jersey, who encouraged me to keep writing. Much love to my children, Leonard, Sharonda, Qiana and Lawrence and my four grandchildren. And finally, a humble thank you to the black Pentecostal church as a whole, for teaching me the way I should go, and now that I am old, I will not depart from it. Love, Sister Sharon.

Printed in the United States
By Bookmasters